Book1: Deliver Me From Negative Self-talk: A Guide to Speaking Faith-filled

Book 2: Lord Help Me With Negative Emotions: A Guide To Controlling Emotions & Finding Peace In The Midst of Storms

Book 3: Deliver Me from Negative Health Talk: A Guide to Speaking Healing Words of Faith

Book 4: Get Off Your Knees And Do Something About It: 17 Things To Do After You Pray

PUBLISHED BY
Lynn R Davis

Be the first to know when my books are free. Visit: LynnRDavis.com today to register your email address.

Copyright © 2013 All rights reserved.
No part of this publication may be copied, reproduced in any format, by any means, electronic or otherwise, without prior consent from the copyright owner and publisher of this book.

Book 1

Deliver Me from Negative Self Talk

A Guide to Speaking Faith-filled Words

Lynn R. Davis

PUBLISHED BY
Lynn R Davis

Be the first to know when my books are free. Visit: LynnRDavis.com today to register your email address.

Copyright © 2013 All rights reserved.
No part of this publication may be copied, reproduced in any format, by any means, electronic or otherwise, without prior consent from the copyright owner and publisher of this book.

Table of Contents

Preface

Introduction:

1- Words You Should Never Speak About Yourself

2- Words You Should Never Speak About Others

3- Words You Should Never Allow Others to Speak About You

4- Words You Should Never Speak About God

5- Knowing God's Loving Character

6- Daily Inspiration and Scripture Meditation

Popular Articles - Bonus Chapter

Other Books by Lynn R. Davis

Preface

Satan deliberately attacked Job's family, his possessions, and his physical health.

Sometimes the problems we face are direct attacks from the enemy. But other times, we have ourselves to blame. We curse ourselves by speaking words of doom and death.

Words should be chosen carefully, because they have power to give life and to destroy it.

Negative self-talk is conceived in the mind and birthed through our speech. But just as negative seeds produce a negative harvest, so will the seeds of God's word, planted in a faithful heart, produce an abundant harvest of blessings.

Introduction:

Proverbs 18: 21 says, "Life and death are in the power of the tongue." Simply put, our words will either give life or cause death. Where did we get this powerful gift?

From our Father that's where. Just as God created the heavens and the earth by speaking words, we too can create the life we desire for ourselves.

Here's an easy formula to remember:

MEDITATION + DECLARATION = MANIFESTATION

If you want something to happen in your life, speak it into existence and then act on your faith. Instead of talking about how terrible your relationship is, confess that the relationship is Godly and all is well.

Does this mean that you can "name it and claim it?" No that's not what I am saying at all. There is more to breakthrough and manifestation than claiming it. What I am encouraging you to do is believe. Believe that God wants you to live a blessed and victorious life at whatever level you are.

Believe that God still can and will do miracles. Believe that God loves you enough to care about what you are going through and will move on your behalf if you have faith to believe.

Your words matter. Your thoughts matter. Your actions are crucial. This book covers your speech. It deals with the negative thoughts that bombard your mind when you're going through hell, your friends and family are MIA, and you can't see how you're going to make it.

The negative thoughts tempt you to say what you see. I'm asking you to challenge yourself. Don't say what you see, declare what you desire.

If you want something to manifest in your life, you have the power to speak it into existence. The opposite is also true. The things that you don't want in your life can also manifested because of your continuous negative self-talk. Instead of talking about how terrible your life is or how miserable your relationship is, why not say what you want? Why not confess that your partner has a Godly attitude and all is well?

Shift your focus from your problem to God's promises. Faith pleases God (Hebrews 11:6). And your faith comes by hearing the word of God (Romans 10:17).

Be Careful What You Say

We are made in the image of God and "By the word of the LORD were the heavens made; and all the host of them by the breath of his." (Psalm 33:6)

"Through faith we understand that the worlds were framed by the word of God, so that things which are seen were not made of things which do." (Hebrews 11:3)

The words you speak create the world that you experience. That's why it's important to bridal your tongue especially when you're angry.

When you are upset or angry, resist the temptation to feed the fire of doom with negative words. No matter how broke you are, don't go around saying, "I'm broke." No matter how rebellious your child seems, resist the urge to say, "You're hopeless!"

Instead, when you face financial challenges say, "All of my needs are met in Jesus' name." When you speak what you want, you are calling it into existence.

Each time your child rebels, administer discipline in love and declare, "The seed of the righteous is blessed!"

Even though it seems that nothing is happening in the natural world, things are changing in the spirit realm.

Your words are a seed planted in the ground. You can't see what's happening. But the chemistry of the ground is changing and the seed is germinating.

Don't get discouraged because you can't see a change in your finances right away. Don't revert to negative self-talk because your child misses curfew again.

Take a deep breath. Know that God is moving. Your faith is pleasing Him and things will change. And like the blossom breaks through the surface of the ground, your prayers will be answered and a breakthrough will spring forth.

And it's only a matter of time before your situation improves. "Calling those things that be not as though they were," is a biblical principal.

Don't be misled. Time is a factor. You don't plant a seed today and see a sprout tomorrow. You've begun a process and that process takes place in stages as described in the Mark 4 Parable of the Sower: "first the blade, then the ear, after that the full corn in the ear."

You have been given the power to sow words and reap a harvest of whatever you have sown. That is why we should be very careful what we say and how we respond to the challenges in our lives.

Once we realize the seriousness of our words, we begin to choose them more carefully. Okay, now that we have our own words under control, let's discuss the next important issue; the words that other people say to us.

Sticks And Stones Break Bones And Words Do Hurt!

Most of the words we hear seem innocent and even humorous. But remember what we said before; words either give life or cause death.

"Sticks and stones may break my bones, but words will never hurt me."

We said it all the time as kids. But the truth is; words *can* hurt. At work I was sharing with a co-worker how I had just been diagnosed with high blood pressure.

His immediate response was, "Be careful. You could stroke out and die." At first I laughed it off. "Boy you're so crazy."

But later that day, I started thinking about what he said. It was true that extreme stress could increase blood pressure and even lead to a stroke.

Had I been experiencing a little numbness - maybe even a little fatigue and dizziness? The negative thoughts started running rampant in my mind.

Honestly, before hearing my friend's "words of wisdom." emphasis on "***dom;***" having a stroke had never entered my mind before he spoke the words.

I meditated on his negativity, and *voilà*! I started experiencing symptoms. Ever heard of hypochondria?

The American Century Dictionary defines it as an abnormal anxiety about one's health.

My grandmother was accused of being a hypochondriac. She was always experiencing multiple types of illnesses.

Even though doctors couldn't find anything wrong; bottles of prescriptions lined her dresser. Eighty percent of her day was spent in bed.

Granny only got out of the house for doctor's appointments. Friends and neighbors visited with their stories of doom and gloom. Their words were feeding her fear of death by illness.

If only she had known the power that she had within her to speak health and healing into her life, to control her anxiety, and call forth a sound mind and peace.

Granny had the fiery darts of negativity shooting at her from all directions-both from within and from the gloomy people around her.

What's my point? She meditated on the thoughts and like seeds they took root and produced fear. The fear produced doubt. And doubt murders faith.

The constant meditating on negativity lead to her taking multiple medications, but never to her being healed. As believers we must not allow negativity to overcome us.

Read Paul's instructions to the church: "For the weapons of our warfare are not carnal but mighty in God for pulling down strongholds, casting down arguments and every high thing that exalts itself against the knowledge of God and to bring every thought into captivity" 2 Cor. 10:4-5.

We have to capture bad thoughts and control them with the word of God. The only way to win a spiritual battle is to fight it using spiritual weapons.

"(3) We are human, but we don't wage war as humans do. (4) We use God's mighty weapons, not worldly weapons, to knock down the strongholds of human reasoning and to destroy false arguments." (2 Cor. 10 NLV)

If I hadn't come to myself and remembered that Jesus died that I might have life, I would have meditated my way right into a stroke.

How could this happen?

MEDITATION + DECLARATION = MANIFESTATION

It's a process. First, you see or hear something negative. Next, you think about it or meditate on it (too long).

Then, you start speaking about the negative thing you saw or heard. Finally, the negativity overcomes you and you begin to feel like there is no hope.

No Matter How Bad It Looks Stay Positive

Let's say you're having relationship issues. Like most people, you want to vent. So you talk to your friends about your situation. Of course, as your friends, they're going to take your side.

They begin to say negative things about your situation like, "She's never going to change," "Just leave," "You deserve better." All of these seeds are planted in your mind just waiting to be watered with fear so that they can grow and produce division and dissolution.

You've now developed a totally pessimistic attitude toward that person and your relationship. And if you allow this to go on, the situation will end in pain. What will you do?

Will you fight with spiritual weapons or will you lay down in defeat? You could respond either way.

But let's look at the spiritual approach. First recognize that Satan hates unity and is working to destroy your relationship. Why does he hate unity?

Because God blesses unity!

Read Psalms 133:1-3. "(v1) Behold how good and how pleasant it is for brethren to dwell together in unity. (v3) It is like the dew of Hermon Descending upon the mountains of Zion' for there the Lord commanded the blessing-Life forevermore."

We've looked at the spiritual approach. So maybe you're wondering what the negative approach look like? Here goes:

You hear your friend's words. You worry about the negative aspects of your relationship. You start speaking negatively. Your relationship ends.

Short and sweet-once again-whatever you meditate on will manifest. Revisit the formula:

MEDITATION+ DECLARATION= MANIFESTATION.

That's why God wants us to meditate on His word day and night. And Romans 10:17 tells us that "faith comes by hearing, and hearing by the word of God."

Make God's Words Your Words

As believers, we must speak only words of prosperity, health, and power. It takes some practice. But it can be done. Study the word and meditate on God's promises.

Soon, instead of words of despair flowing from your lips, you will begin to flood your life with God's perfect will! And what started out as practice will be as common as breathing!

Say the formula aloud:

MEDITATION + DECLARATION= MANIFESTATION

1- Words You Should Never Speak About Yourself

Admit it. You talk to yourself.

I talk to myself all the time. I especially do it when I'm zooming around the house. I remind myself, "don't forget the fabric softener" or scold myself, "Lynn, you put it on the list and still forgot to buy it!"

Of course, these are some of the nicer conversations I have with myself.

And most of the time, self talk is pretty harmless. No one gets offended and nobody gets hurt.

But when a situation is more serious than staticky underwear or crusty oven racks, things change; the voices of panic and fear take over.

Like the day you blow a job interview, lose a loved one, or get devastating news from the doctor. The voices change and innocent self talk turns negative and critical.

We make comments like, "I give up. I can't do it," "I can't go on without them," and "I'll be dead in six months."

Negative thoughts are spiritually impure and must be filtered. The word of God is your filter. Any such thought that makes you feel defeated, hurt, or insufficient is a **LIE** and must be filtered through the word of God.

Study for knowledge. Seek understanding. Pray for wisdom. Find out what the bible says about your situation. Remember, "Seek and you will find."

Your goal is to get to the truth. It is the truth that will set you free!

Your Personal Speaking Guide

Don't say: My entire body aches. I'm just falling apart!
Do Say: Sickness and disease shall not lord over me.

Don't say: I am so exhausted. I really don't feel like doing anything today.
Do Say: I can do all things through Christ who strengthens me

Don't say: This headache is killing me!
Do Say: Headache, I resist you in the name of Jesus and by his stripes I am healed and made whole.

Don't say: I can't do that. I'm too scared. What if I fail?
Do Say: I am courageous. God has not given me a spirit of fear but of a sound mind, power and love.

Don't say: I'm always broke.
Do Say: I am abundantly supplied. God is supplying all of my needs according to his riches in glory.

Don't say: I am so depressed.
Do Say: I have the mind of Christ and the peace of God that surpasses all understanding.

Don't say: I just can't stop this bad habit.
Do Say: I am not tempted or tried above that which I am able to overcome. I am more than a conqueror.

Don't say: Everyone in my family has this problem. It's hereditary, so I will probably have the same problems

too.
Do Say: Christ redeemed me from the curse, being made a curse himself. I am delivered out of every affliction.

Don't say: I don't like people. I'd rather be alone, besides people are mean.
Do Say: I have the compassion of Christ in my heart and I love all people.

Don't say: I'll never meet this deadline. My work is overwhelming me, there's no way that I can meet the demands of this job.
Do Say: I have the grace to overcome every obstacle. God is giving me wisdom to solve every problem that I am faced with.

Don't Say: I'm happy with what I have. Why should I want more?
Do Say: Jesus came that I might have abundant life. I am blessed to be a blessing to others.

Don't say: I will never get married. No one wants to marry me.
Do Say: God is preparing me for marriage and he is raising up the perfect mate for me.

Don't Say: God is not answering my prayers so maybe he's not listening.
Do Say: God is mindful of me and he hears me when I pray.

Don't Say: Everything is getting on my nerves and I am going crazy!
Do Say: I will think only of things that are lovely, good, just, and have good report so that the peace of God dwells in me.

Don't say: I'm so angry. I will never be able to forgive.
Do Say: The joy of the Lord is my strength. My heart is filled with the compassion of Christ and I forgive those who trespass against me.

Don't say: My company is going to have a reduction in force. I don't know what I'm going to do if I get laid off.
Do Say: When one door closes God has to open another door.

Don't say: I am lonely. I wish I had someone to in my life.
Do Say: I am complete in Christ. I am never lonely because he is always with me.

Don't say: Things will never get better. I may as well give up.
Do Say: Eyes haven't seen what God has prepared for me and in due season I shall reap, if I faint not.

Don't say: The weather is terrible. I hope I don't have an accident.
Do Say: The angels of the Lord are encamped around me and no hurt or harm shall come near me.

Don't say: I'm too old to change. You can't teach old dogs new tricks.
Do Say: I am a new creature. Old things have passed away.

Don't Say: Everyone else is doing it, why shouldn't I?
Do Say: God has called me out of darkness and into his marvelous light. I am in this world but I am not of this world.

Don't say: I can't help gossiping. My friends encourage it.

Do Say: I will not participate in gossip. Corrupt communication brings destruction.

Don't say: No one cares about me!
Do Say: God loves me and he is Jehovah-Shammah (The Lord Is There)

2-Words You Should Never Speak About Others

As a mother of a recovering addict, I know this principle is a tough one. When I first found out that my son was smoking pot in high school I lost it.

I used words I've never used in my life. I was so angry you could have fried on egg on my head!

I was disappointed in him. Angry that I'd missed the signs and appalled that the enemy had the nerve to go after my child. Not my son! (Maybe that's a book for another time.)

Every chance I got I shared my disgust and contempt for his rebellion. I told family and coworkers how much trouble he was getting into and how many times he'd been arrested.

I complained and lamented till I was out of breath, then had the nerve to pray to God for change. What I should have been doing was praying for him, with him, and speaking words of promise over his life. While keeping my mouth closed about what was happening.

The more negatively I spoke about his habits and his choices, the more he backed away from me and toward the rebellion. It wasn't until I took my negative thoughts into captivity and changed my words, that I began to see change and have been blessed to witness his deliverance.

Learn from my mistakes. Don't speak negativity over the people in your life. If you truly care about them and want to reconcile the relationship, replace your negative perceptions and comments with the word of God.

Remember, **"For our struggle is not against human opponents, but against rulers, authorities, cosmic powers in the darkness around us..."** (Ephesians 6:12)

Your Personal Speaking Guide

Don't say: My supervisor hates me, my co-workers are messy; I hate this job!
Do Say: I love those who hate me and I will do well to those who misuse me. No weapon formed against me shall prosper. The battle is the Lord's.

Don't say: My children do not listen to a word that I say. They are just bad.
Do Say: My child is a blessing from the lord. My child obeys the word of God and honors his mother and father.

Don't say: My husband is lazy and worthless. I don't know why I married him.
Do Say: My husband is a righteous man of God and he loves me like Christ loves the church.

Don't say: My in-laws are incorrigible and they are making my life miserable.
Do Say: My in-laws are transformed by the renewing of their mind. I am an example for them and they will see my good works and glorify the Father in heaven.

Don't say: People in church are cruel. I'm never going to church again.
Do Say: God has many great churches and he is revealing to me the church that I should attend.

Don't say: My child makes terrible grades in school. They will never amount to anything.
Do Say: God has a purpose for my child. My child is royal priesthood and has the wisdom of Daniel and the favor of God and man. My child is empowered to prosper.

Don't Say: Why do they behave that way? They're just crazy.
Do Say: Christ alone is perfect.

3- Words You Should Never Allow Others to Speak About You

Some people are just plain negative. That's all there is to it. But you don't have to allow them to discourage you. Regardless of who they are or how close they may be to us.

Sometimes the people closest to you are the ones who will be the least supportive and the most negative.

You're all excited about your new goal and you share it with your significant other, brother, sister, or BFF and you're met with negativity.

That's the last thing you expected. How are you supposed to process that? What do you do?

You ignore negative people. That's what you do.

I deal with people and their toxic comments all the time regarding my health and weight loss goals.

Anyone who knows me is aware that I'm an advocate of health and fitness. You would think people would appreciate that, right?

Wrong!

I hear comments all the time like, "You're going to be too skinny." "You don't need to lose weight," or "I can't eat like that. I love food too much," on and on...

Did I let that stop me from dropping 4 jean sizes and getting healthy? No. I did not. And I will not. I prefer not spending hundreds of dollars a year on high blood pressure pills and asthma pumps - thank you very much.

You see, I'm fully aware that negative people are speaking from the depths of their own insecurity and self-doubt.

So I brush it off.

That's what I want to encourage you to do as well. When you decide to improve yourself, there will be people who will say and do things to discourage you.

I encourage you to shake those negative people off. Realize they are only projecting their lack of discipline and lack of motivation on to you.

"Hurting people hurt people." I don't know who said that, but it is certainly a true statement.

Some people are unhappy with themselves and they're jealous of your drive and commitment to self-improvement. *How dare you improve your quality of life? Who do you think you are?*

You can't please negative people. They are unhappy no matter what. They speak negatively no matter what. They gossip about you when you fail and they rain on your parade when you succeed.

There's no pleasing them. So stop trying! Simply smile and keep it moving.

You have goals. Don't let negative people deter you. Stay focused and you will succeed.

"Let no corrupt communication proceed out of your mouth, but that which is good to the use of edifying, that it may minister grace unto the hearers." (Ephesians 4:29)

If the words that people are speaking over you don't uplift you or encourage you to do better, then you should never receive them as truth.

Your Personal Speaking Guide

What they say: You poor thing.
Response: I am blessed and I have the grace to overcome anything!

What they say: How do you plan to acquire that? You don't make enough.
Response: I am abundantly supplied. I am not moved by what I see. It's only temporary.

What they say: That's a terrible sickness; you could die from it.
Response: I am healed. I shall live and not die.

What they say: You don't look well. Are you sick?
Response: I have divine health. I resist sickness in the name of Jesus.

What they say: Yeah right, do you really believe you're going to pull that off?
Response: I can do all things through Christ who strengthens me.

What they say: If I were you, I would be so depressed.
Response: God has not given me the spirit of fear, but of a sound mind, power, and love.

What they say: I could never give that much money to the church. I have bills to pay.
Response: When I give, God causes men to give to me, good measure, press down, shaken together and

running over. God supplies all of my needs according to his riches in glory.

What they say: I don't believe in anything that I can't see.
Response: Without faith it is impossible to please God. I receive the promised of God through faith.

What they say: Don't you get tired of cooking, cleaning and taking care of everyone else?
Response: I have the grace to care for the family that God has blessed me with.

4-Words You Should Never Speak About God

God Is Not Angry With You

One of the most difficult things for us to believe as Christians is that God is not mad at us. We condemn ourselves because of our past sins or even our present mistakes.

The danger in believing that you serve an **angry God** is that you will begin to feel you do not deserve God's goodness or His blessings. In turn you will begin to doubt and have fear.

While we don't condone sin or even encourage it, we do know that the bible tells us in Romans 8 "... *there is no condemnation for those who belong to Christ Jesus...*"

I posted a word of encouragement on my Facebook page that I believe applies to this chapter...

"Regardless of disagreements among siblings and

family, when an outsider threatens a family member, we rise against that attacker to protect them. Though your actions don't always please God, when the enemy threatens to destroy you, God raises a standard against him to protect you. You have protection. Not because you do everything right, but because you are in God's family. Receive it by faith."

You are part of the family of God. He loves you and wants to protect you. Here are some daily confessions based on Romans 8 and Isaiah 54.

Meditating on these truths will help you to address your feelings of condemnation and fears of inadequacy because you incorrectly believe that God is angry with you:

- I have an unconditional covenant with God.
- God loves me and He has reconciled me unto himself.
- God is not angry with me. He loves me.
- The mountains and the hills will pass away before God's covenant promise to love me and give me peace can ever be broken.
- God has sworn never to rebuke me or to be angry with me.
- God's covenant of peace will never leave me.
- God's unfailing love and peace for me will never be shaken.
- My righteousness is of the Lord. I am not condemned. I am loved by God.
- Make these confessions daily and know that God loves you regardless of your past, present, or future mistakes. Seek to do good and please Him with your life.

Allow His love to fill your heart and overflow in your life. You do not serve an angry God.

Meditate on Isaiah 54: 10, "Though the mountains be shaken and the hills be removed, yet my unfailing love for you will not be shaken nor my covenant of peace be removed, says the LORD, who has compassion on you." NIV

You serve a loving God. Hills will be removed and mountains shaken before God's love will ever be taken away from you or His covenant with you broken. Believe that. Receive it and walk in victory.

That said, here are a few examples of words you should never speak about God.

- God Doesn't Love Me.
- God is too busy for my problems.
- My problems are too big for God.
- I'm alone. God is not there.
- God can't heal my disease.
- God is going to punish me for my sins.

These are lies, lies, lies; all lies.

The Devil is a liar. He is the "Father of Lies" (John 8:44)

Satan is destined to eternal damnation. He is damned. And he wants to take as many lost souls with him as he possibly can.

Don't let the bad things in life make you believe God

doesn't love you.

God is love. And God loves us-with all of our issues and faults. Jehovah is not waiting to condemn you or to punish you. He wants to bless you.

He's waiting to help you and heal the hurt. It doesn't matter how much wrong you've done. Or how many mistakes you've made or will make.

He only wants to bless you. He is mindful of you and no human could ever love you as much as He does!

God is your provider, peace, and healer. He wants the best for you. And you have to get into the habit of talking like it.

One thing that will help is meditating on the names of God. Learning who He is will help you understand His character and how much He loves and wants you to succeed in life.

5- Knowing God's Loving Character

"O LORD, our Lord, How excellent is Your name in all the earth..." Psalm 8:1

When you know who God is, you can't help but feel comforted and empowered. Everything that you could possibly need is in the Father.

He IS whatever you need Him to be. And He is waiting for you to come to Him.

Whatever you need, God IS! God told Moses in Exodus, "I am that I am." Don't put limits on God's ability to heal your body or repair your broken heart.

God loves you and wants you to be prosperous in every area of your life.

Before you allow someone to tell you that God doesn't love you or that He cannot help you, remember the words, "I am that I am."

He is love, provision, protection, peace, healing, etc. The list goes on and on. Let's take a look at some of the most common characteristics of God our Father:

Names of Jehovah God

Adonai: My Master

El Elyon: The Most High God

El Olam: The Everlasting Father

El Roi: My God Sees All

El Shaddai: My All-Sufficient God

Elohim: My Creator

Jehovah-Jireh: The LORD my Provider

Jehovah-Mekoddishkem: The LORD Who sanctifies me

Jehovah-Nissi: The LORD My Banner

Jehovah-Raah: The LORD My Shepherd

Jehovah-Rapha: The LORD That Heals me

Jehovah-Sabaoth: The LORD of Hosts

Jehovah-Shalom: The LORD my Peace

Jehovah-Shammah: The LORD Is Always There

Jehovah-Tsidkenu: The LORD my Righteousness

God is your creator. He loves you. He wants to provide for you. His desire is to heal you and bring you peace in your storms.

You are righteous because of His son Jesus. And He is always with you even at this moment.

There is no need to speak doom and gloom. God has a good plan for your life. The problems you are facing come from the enemy, not the Father (Jeremiah 29:11).

When you know God, you know His nature. By nature, God is love. And that love is unconditional for believers in Jesus Christ.

I hope that you've been blessed. And I could say that this is the end, but it's not; it's only the beginning. Go forth. "Call those things that be not as though they were." (Romans 4:17)

Choose your words carefully from this day forward. Use them to create a life that you enjoy living.

Remember:

MEDITATION + DECLARATION= MANIFESTATION

Dismiss negative thoughts, words, and feelings. Study your Father's character. Meditate on His word. Declare it. And watch your life change for the better.

6-Daily Inspiration and Scripture Meditation

Ever heard the saying, "What's in you will come out?" It's a true saying.

The only way that we can consistently speak faith-filled words is if those words are "in us" or abundant in our hearts. Matthew 12:34, "For out of the abundance of the heart the mouth speaks."

And for God's word to flourish in our hearts, we must sow seeds of the word through daily prayer, mediation, and study.

The word of God in our hearts takes root and produces a bumper crop of manifestation and breakthrough. So that when we open our mouths to speak, faith-filled words will overflow from it.

Actively seek God's guidance and practice speaking faith-filled words daily. It may feel forced or "fake" at first. And you may be tempted to give up, but please don't.

The pages that follow include 7 days of inspiration and scripture meditation. During your study time meditate on them and pray for understanding.

Ask the Holy Spirit to reveal the value and meaning to you for your life and to show you the areas you need to strengthen.

Matthew 7: 7 - *"Ask, and it shall be given you; seek, and ye shall find; knock, and it shall be opened unto you:"*

DAY 1

Scripture Meditation:

Proverbs 18:21 - "Death and life are in the power of the tongue: and they that love it shall eat the fruit thereof."

Thought for today:

Your words can kill or give life. And there are consequences for both. Today make an effort to speak words that give life and hope for a new beginning to a coworker, friend or family member.

Inspirational Quote:

"A helping word to one in trouble is often like a switch on a railroad track an inch between wreck and smooth, rolling prosperity."

-Henry Ward Beecher

DAY 2

Scripture Meditation:

Proverbs 21:23(NLT) - "Watch your tongue and keep your mouth shut, and you will stay out of trouble."

Thought for today:

If you can't say something nice, don't say anything at all." We don't always have to talk. Sometimes, it's better to keep quiet, especially to avoid starting trouble. If your words will cause confusion don't just blurt them out. Let the Holy Spirit guide you. "God is not the author of confusion but of peace." (1 Corinthians 14:33).

Inspirational Quote:

"If a sudden jar can cause me to speak an impatient, unloving word, then I know nothing of Calvary love. For a cup brimful of sweet water cannot spill even one drop of bitter water, however suddenly jolted."

-Amy Carmichael

DAY 3

Scripture Meditation:

1 Corinthians 2:16 (NLT) - "Who can know the Lord's thoughts? Who knows enough to teach them? But we understand these things, for we have the mind of Christ."

Thought for today:

As a believer you have access to God's thoughts- through His Son, His word and His Spirit. As we spend time with God, our relationship with Him matures. And we begin to gain insight and understanding concerning His good plans for our lives. Pray and believe for the mind of Christ. Then allow God's thoughts to lead your actions.

Inspirational Quote:

"We need men so possessed by the Spirit of God that God can think His thoughts through our minds, that He can plan His will through our actions, that He can direct His strategy of world evangelization through His Church."

-Alan Redpath

DAY 4

Scripture Mediation:

Matthew 21:22 (ESV) - "And whatever you ask in prayer, you will receive, if you have faith."

Thought for today:

There will be times when it seems impossible to overcome what you face. With God nothing is impossible. Your faith is the key to overcoming. Don't mediate on doubtful thoughts or speak doubtful words. Doubt turns to unbelief. And it is unbelief that drives a wedge between you and your promised victory. Stand fast on God's word. His word cannot fail.

Inspirational Quote:

"Daily living by faith on Christ is what makes the difference between the sickly and the healthy Christian, between the defeated and the victorious saint."

-A.W.Pink

DAY 5

Scripture Meditation:

Joshua 1: 8 - "This Book of the Law shall not depart from your mouth, but you shall meditate on it day and night, so that you may be careful to do according to all that is written in it. For then you will make your way prosperous, and then you will have good success."

Thought for today:

We are no longer under the law, but covered by grace. However, I believe the principle is that we should not make the mistake of waiting for God to bring us success. He has already blessed us with the greatest success conduit - His son Jesus Christ. To receive the success that is promised to us we must first receive Jesus into our lives as Lord and savior. Then by faith believe that we have also received salvation, healing, prosperity, and wholeness. Meditate on the promises in God's word. Learn them. Believe them. Declare them. And then you "will have good success."

Inspirational Quote:

"The foundation stones for a balanced success are honesty, character, integrity, faith, love and loyalty."

-Zig Ziglar

Day 6

Scripture Meditation:

Isaiah 26:3 – 4 - "You keep him in perfect peace whose mind is stayed on you, because he trusts in you. Trust in the Lord forever, for the Lord God is an everlasting rock:"

Thought for today:

As the hymn says, we often forfeit our peace because we fail to take our problems to God. God wants us to cast our cares on him. Not our unbelieving neighbors, disgruntled coworkers, or pessimistic family members. Though everything around you seems to be falling apart, take heart in knowing that God's word is not. It is solid as an everlasting rock. His word and His love will never fade. He is a part of you. And that part of you is indestructible. It's the part of your life that rebuilds, restores, and resurrects! Nothing is impossible with God.

Inspirational Scripture:

"You were made by God and for God and until you understand that, life will never make sense."

Rick Warren

Day 7

Scripture Meditation:

1 John 4:4 - "Because greater is He that is in you than He that is in the world."

Thought for today:

The word and Jesus are one. "In the beginning was the word. The word was God and the word was with God." (John 1:1) Jesus lives in you. And He that lives in you is greater and more powerful than any obstacle you face in the world. Don't look down at your problems. Look up at the promise. Your help comes from the Lord and He is high and lifted up, just as your countenance should be. Keep your head up.

Inspirational Quote:

"If there be anything that can render the soul calm, dissipate its scruples and dispel its fears, sweeten its sufferings by the anointing of love, impart strength to all its actions, and spread abroad the joy of the Holy Spirit in its countenance and words, it is this simple and childlike repose in the arms of God."

-S.D. Gordon

END

If you enjoyed this book and think the message should be spread, please do me a favor by taking a moment to leave your honest feedback on Amazon.com.

BOOK #2

Lord, Help Me With My Negative Emotions:

A Guide To Controlling Your Emotions And Finding Peace In The Midst of Storms

(Deliverance Series)

PUBLISHED BY: Lynn R Davis

Be the first to know when my books are free. Visit: LynnRDavis.com today to register your email address.

Copyright © 2014 All rights reserved.

No part of this publication may be copied, reproduced in any format, by any means, electronic or otherwise, without prior consent from the copyright owner and publisher of this book.

Table of Contents

1 Control Your Emotions Or They Will Control You

2 Second Hand Stress

3 Deliver Me From Misery Loves Company

4 Managing Negative Emotions: Anger, Anxiety, And Depression

5 Finding True Happiness

6 Inspirational Quotes About Emotions

Introduction

Emotional bondage is the worst type slavery. Every negative circumstance becomes your master. Whenever something or someone triggers your negative reaction, you become like a puppet on a string. Your feelings easily manipulate you into behaving in a way that only hurts you and the people around you. It's time for a change.

Is this book for you? Here's how you can tell. You, or someone you know, responds to negative people or circumstances by:

**Sobbing until your head hurts

**Going off

**Losing it

**Throwing a fit

** Breaking things

**Yelling

**Hitting

**Seeking revenge at all cost

**Slashing tires

**Pulling out a pistol

**Becoming depressed

**Losing sleep

If any of those sound like you, then you should take steps today to change how you handle your negative emotions. There is an alternative positive response for every negative emotion you face. I know many will disagree with this particular work because we have accepted that our environment, people, and circumstances control our emotions. And because of that, our emotional responses can only improve when our environment improves. I disagree.

Based on personal experience, I believe it's possible to respond positively in the most negative of situations. Having experienced the big D's in my life: Death, Divorce, and Depression, I fully understand emotional pain. In every instance, I felt like crawling under a rock and never coming out again. But I came out from under the rock. I smiled again. I loved again. I lived life again.

Take Paul and Silas, when they were locked in prison. They chose to sing and pray rather than lament and lose emotional control. There are many other Biblical examples and we will look at some of them in this book. Like these great examples, I believe we too can keep our cool and not fall apart every time our environment falls apart.

I'm not saying that I never sought professional help. Before I got my emotions under control, I took anti-depressants for a short time. Some people will need professional help and they should not feel ashamed about seeking it. What I am saying is, the "help" I received wasn't what delivered me. I believe my ability to overcome was the result of faith. It was God's love that brought me out of the darkness of depression and back into the light of His love and acceptance.

This book is for people who have tried and failed at controlling emotions but aren't ready to give up.

Use this scripture as a mantra:

Psalm 34:19 says, "*Many are the afflictions of the righteous, but the LORD delivers him out of them all.*"

Plug in the word *emotional* right before *afflictions* and read it again:

> *Many are the [emotional] afflictions of the righteous, but the LORD delivers him out of them all.*

Now, ask God to help you believe that you are emotionally healed.

Chapter 1: Control Your Emotions or They Will Control You

"What worries you, masters you."- unknown

The Power Of Your Emotions

When emotions are uncontrolled, they wreak havoc. It only takes seconds for an outburst of negative emotion to tear a relationship to shreds. If allowed, damaging emotions like jealousy, anger, or insecurity will take control and burn like wild fire.

I remember, years ago, when I found out my ex was cheating. My emotions ranged from sadness and depression to jealousy and rage. I thought about throwing all his clothes into the courtyard of our complex. Then, I contemplated calling all of his family and friends and telling them what a lying, cheating jerk I saw him as. Worse still, I wanted to face the other woman and let her have it! I was ticked off and I was ready to play judge and jury.

I was confused. I wondered what I had done wrong. My emotions were all over the place. Now, years later, when I think about it, I'm amazed that I came out of that situation in one piece. It was hard. It hurt like heck, but I'm here to tell you about it. I survived and so can you.

One of the keys to controlling emotions is knowing that you don't have to be at the mercy of your circumstance or situation. The natural tendency is to overreact or respond in ways that do more harm than good. Sure, in the short term, you feel vindicated, but if you truly are a man or woman of God, you can never be at peace with acting out of retaliation or vengeance.

Uncontrolled negative emotions can often lead to heated arguments, or worse. We've all seen the horrible true stories on crime TV of people whose emotions got the best of them. And then later, in the interviews, they wish they'd just walked away or made some other decision.

Think of a time when you were in a bad situation. Or maybe you're in one now. Did you have trouble controlling your emotions then? Are you having trouble right now controlling your emotions, even though you know you should?

God doesn't want you to suffer. He doesn't want you to hurt yourself or anyone else. He knows you are hurting. He knows you want to feel vindicated. But He doesn't want you to make the situation worse. He doesn't want to see you suffer more than you are in this moment. So He's encouraging you to take control. Try to detach yourself from the negative emotion and re-attach yourself to His word.

> *Many are the [**emotional**] afflictions of the righteous, but the LORD delivers him out of them all.*

Do something to take your mind off the situation. Read your Bible. Watch your favorite televangelist. Listen to music. Go for a walk to clear your head. And if you need to cry, cry. If you just have to talk to someone, call a trusted mentor or person you *really* trust. Someone who will help you keep a level head. The last person you need to contact is an emotionally charged acquaintance who slashes tires and keys cars. You can come out on top, even if you cry buckets of tears and feel like your heart is shattered. God heals and His Son comforts us. "In the world you have tribulation, but take courage; *I have overcome the world.*" (John 16:33) With everything I was faced with, shame, embarrassment, fear of loneliness, betrayal, etc., I still worked hard to control the negative emotions that bombarded me constantly. I didn't go all Angela Basset from *Waiting to Exhale* or Sandra Bullock from *Hope Floats*. Yes, I yelled at him. And I most certainly told him a thing or two about himself. I was hurt and, quite honestly, I wanted him to suffer.

I didn't think I would ever be able to forgive him or the other woman. But I kept my composure. I remembered God's word, *"The LORD is near to the brokenhearted and saves the crushed in spirit." (Psalm 34:18)* I asked

God to handle it and I trusted Him to keep his promise. It took months and months for me to get over the pain. But I did. I began to notice that it didn't hurt as much. And, one day, I woke up with the memory but the pain was gone. Today, he and I can laugh and talk without rehearsing the past. The Lord really does heal broken hearts.

Emotions Can Help You And Hinder You. To be successful and competent, in personal and professional relationships, you have to be able to control emotions. More often than not, you will be judged based on your ability to deal with emotions, especially in difficult times. People who are able to keep their emotions in check, even when the chips are down, advance further in life, personally, professionally, and spiritually. Emotions aren't all bad. Anger and fear are very strong emotions. In scripture, we repeatedly see "fear not". But in regard to anger, we are told, "Be angry but sin not." I think that's because fear is more of a debilitating emotion. It opens the door for doubt. And our faith doesn't work when we doubt. Fear tends to stop me in my tracks whereas anger, when controlled, motivates me to change or improve. When my marriage ended, I was angry that I had to start over, move in with my dad, and pay a pile of debts. But I directed that anger toward improving my situation. I applied to graduate school, created a debt management plan, and eventually was able to purchase a home.

My trust in God kept the fear at bay. My faith helped me control and redirect my anger toward solving my problems rather than creating more. We really do have to make the choice to control our emotions. No matter how stressed or pressured we become, we can't let our environment threaten our emotional stability or how we react under pressure.

I had a manager once who was super good at what he did. We worked in a small group but were responsible for managing project resources for hundreds of employees that equated to millions of dollars. The job was stressful at times. Although our manager was good at budgeting and resource management, he had a tendency to fly off the handle when things went wrong. Whenever there was a problem with the reports or numbers, we knew that someone would be yelled at. We'd witnessed more than one employee leaving his office in tears.

This went on for almost a year before I finally found a position elsewhere. Not long after, I ran into one of my ex-team members in the cafeteria. She was grinning from ear to ear. Apparently that manager had been fired because of a formal complaint that was filed about his uncontrolled temper. The company saw him as a liability. She went on to say that he'd been fired from other jobs and passed over for promotions because of his temper. Instead of controlling his emotions, he was allowing them to control him. And they were hindering his career.

Our lives are so fast paced and we come across so many different situations in any given day. When we start out, we may have a clear mind and know what we have to achieve to be productive on that day. However, life unfolds before us and before we know it our plans change. In an instant, we are faced with a situation that irritates us, disappoints us, frustrates us, or annoys us. At these moments, it's important to be in control of how we respond. Always remember that no one else is controlling this for you. You might feel that they are "pushing your buttons", but you are ultimately responsible for what happens next.

Emotions are temporary states of mind, don't let them permanently destroy you.

Our emotions have triggers. Meaning, something ignites them. Emotions will take you over if you allow them to, yet, these emotions only strike when triggered. Every day, someone struggles with emotions. Many people find it difficult to manage these emotions.

> ***Strength doesn't come from what you can do. It comes from overcoming the things you once thought you couldn't.***

Some people have medical or mental related complications that pose challenges for them when it comes to controlling emotions. Let me encourage you. If you think you have a medical condition, talk to a healthcare professional. There are many options out there. God created doctors but as I always say, physicians don't have the final word in your healing- God does. But if you feel overwhelmed and think there may be some other issue going on besides stress, talk to someone and at least eliminate the possibility of a medical condition that may require treatment.

Realize that some of the best tools to control your emotions resides inside of you. You can master your emotions by exploring positive self-talk, scripture meditation, prayer, etc. Make it a choice to master the emotional reactions that cause anger, fear, resentment, doubt, and so on. Find ways to limit your exposure to negative triggers and people.

What's On Your Mind?

Our thoughts are the source. That's why 2 Corinthians 10:5 warns us to cast down every thought and imagination that is contrary to the word. Evil thoughts, when pondered, conceive negative emotions and those negative emotions birth unhealthy reactions. But if we heed 2 Corinthians 10:5 and cast that negative thought down and replace it with the word of God, positive emotions are conceived and healthy emotional responses are born instead.

Sometimes, we respond the way society has told us we should respond when we go through a tough time. Society says its okay to be "pissed off" when someone cuts you off in traffic or takes your parking space. It's "acceptable" understandable to verbally abuse others if that's what you experienced growing it. Depression is after the death of a loved one is expected. No one blames us if we become bitter after a bad break up or divorce. You get the point. Society says our situation dictate our emotions. But the word of God says we should be in control of our emotions. Our feelings can't be allowed to control us. **"A fool loses his temper, but a wise man holds it back." Proverbs 29:11**

So if you have these thoughts and ideas that you're supposed to react negatively when certain things happen, then you're going to do just that-react negatively. Take guilt for instance. It's an emotion based in fear. Fear that you've done something so wrong that you cannot be forgiven. That idea goes against the word of God. It's good that you feel something about the wrong that you've done. Let the guilty feeling be a signal that something is or was wrong and should be address. Then you address it. Confess it. And move on.

"There is therefore no condemnation to them who are in Christ Jesus."

(Romans 8:1)

Emotions Don't Have To Dictate Our Actions

Emotions, like the tongue, can bless us or destroy us. Proverbs 18:21 says life and death are in the power of the tongue. The words we speak can give life or cause death. So it's imperative that we choose our words carefully. But, some times more than others, it can be difficult to control our tongues because of our emotions. Proverbs 29:11 says, "A fool gives full vent to his spirit, but a wise man quietly holds it back." This leads me to believe that God considers us wise when we are able to control our emotions. And by doing so, it will be that much easier to control the words that leave our lips.

We can't let our emotions rule us. Emotions can be controlled. We don't have to let them dictate how we respond to the issues in our life. Just because someone breaks your heart doesn't mean you allow negative emotions of depression, defeat, or bitterness overwhelm you. Don't crawl into a ball and let life pass you by. Be thankful that you Mr. or Ms. Wrong are no longer taking up space in your life. You deserve better. And now that they have vacated, you have room in your life for the perfect mate.

God doesn't want us to just go with the flow of whatever emotion we are feeling at any given time. Can you imagine what the world would be like if we all just acted on our emotions? I know there are some schools of thought that tell us to just feel the emotion.

But personally, I've noticed that when I allow myself to "feel" the emotion, I am bombarded with even more negative emotion. And the more I focus on the negative feelings, the worse I feel. There's just nothing good about getting all worked up and upset whenever something doesn't go my way. So I decided a long time ago that I was going to do the opposite of what I felt. Instead of crying my eyes out I was going to laugh. If I wanted to yell, I prayed and spoke calmly instead. Life has been a lot better. I encourage you to try it. When your emotions flair, instead of reacting the way you normally would, do the opposite. Of course your kids may think you've been alien abducted, but hey that's okay. They will come to love and appreciate the new and improved emotionally healthy you.

An example of doing the opposite is what Jesus told us to do in the midst of turmoil, he said, "Be of good cheer," Christ wasn't saying, "Pretend that everything is great." He was telling us things may look bad right now but be joyful because you already have the victory! Then in John 14:1, He encouraged the disciples, "Let not our hearts be troubled." I don't know about you, but I watched the movie, *The Passion of The Christ*, and that made me cry. How in the world could the disciples see it first hand and not be troubled? Yet, that is what Jesus told them. That was His expectation for the. That they not be troubled even though they were having an emotionally gut-wrenching experience. I believe today Jesus is still telling us not to let ourselves become overwhelmed by negative emotions- not to be troubled. And if he's telling us not to allow it, then we must have the power within us to overcome troubled emotions.

We have to stop justifying falling apart.

The way we respond at the beginning of a crisis determines whether or not we win the battle with that circumstance. It's critical that we don't fall apart. Hindsight is 20/20. We often see our emotional breakdown was clearly a mistake after the damage is already done.

Take control at the beginning with the understanding that you have choices when it comes to emotions. That negative emotion that you are feeling is *not* the only emotion you have to feel. When you feel your emotions overtaking you, stop and say, "God told me to rejoice always."

Say this, *"David blessed the Lord at all times and praised God continually. I will bless and praise God at all times. Even when my emotions are tempting me to be negative, I will rejoice!"*

When we go through a challenge in life, we experience a range of thoughts, emotions, and physical effects. The key to successfully dealing with the circumstance is learning to control those thoughts and emotions. Easier said than done? Yes, until you reach the point where your default response is the word of God. As soon as you are hit with a negative emotion, instead of giving in to it, you automatically ask yourself, **"What does God want me to do in this situation?"** He certainly wouldn't slash a boyfriend's tires; hack into a girlfriends email; or punch a rude neighbor's lights out.

Your Emotions aren't wrong or sinful, they're human nature. People can be irritating. And our human nature, the fleshly man is weak. And quite honestly sometimes, we don't feel like doing the right thing. But that's the mediocrity of the flesh. It wants immediate gratification. It wants revenge. And it wants to see somebody suffer-now. The problem is that immediate negative emotional gratification takes a toll on our hearts. It blocks our blessings. And threatens our relationship with the Father.

Lay aside every weight and sin that so easily besets you. Panic, fear, grief, sadness, anger, they all threaten to "easily beset you". Don't let them. If you're living a life of uncontrolled emotions, you're living a mediocre life. And nowhere in scripture does God tell us to live a mediocre existence.

Whether you've just been fired or experienced a bad break up, instead of replaying the every detail of what went wrong, try something different. Make a different choice. Instead of focusing on the bad, find the good. Realize that God has promised to make everything work together for your good. And that He tells us to be of good cheer because He has overcome the world. When you do this, you're casting down negative thoughts and controlling negative emotions. You are not allowing depression, anger, or resentment to set in. You're in control.

Galatians 5:16 -Walk in the spirit and you shall not walk in the flesh. Lust in the Bible isn't always sexual. Lust is a strong overpowering desire. You can have a strong overpowering desire to slap a rude waitress. But that doesn't mean you should. Just because the negative emotion exists doesn't mean it has to be acted upon. Don't indulge lustful thoughts either. Even if you are saying, "I'll never really slap anyone." It's very dangerous to meditate on negativity. You open the door for more negative emotions to enter your mind and heart thereby increasing your chances of doing what you're thinking. Or if you're in a situation where you're sad or upset, mediating on those emotions could lead you to becoming clinically depressed or acting out in a harmful way toward yourself or others.

You're going to have to change how you think about your situation before you can control how you respond to it. Your thoughts control emotions. Actions produce experience and create an environment. As a man thinks, so is he. The Lord will keep him in perfect peace whose mind is stayed on him. Proverbs 23:7 and Isaiah 26:3 You may think that your environment is the driving force behind your negative emotions. But the Lord tells us again and again in scripture to rejoice in tribulation. If we are instructed to rejoice in tribulation, then we must have a choice, right? When posed with a problem, we can decide to fall apart or fall on our knees. We can react negatively or respond positively. Let's end the chapter with a couple of examples:

Negative Emotion Reaction:

I'm all alone. I will never fall in love again. No one loves me. I don't want to live anymore.

Positive Emotional Response:

I will not let my heart be troubled. I believe in the love of God. His love is filling every void in my heart. I believe also in the resurrecting power of Jesus Christ. I am fearfully wonderfully made and I know that God can resurrect a healthy relationship in my life. I rejoice in the Lord always. God is going to work this situation out for my good.

Negative Emotion Reaction:

I don't have job. How am I going to feed my family? I'm going to lose my home. My identity is gone.

Positive Emotional Response:

Promotion comes from God. (Psalm 75:6-7) He is my source and my Jehovah Jireh. He will provide. I am God's masterpiece (Ephesians 2:10). My identity is in Christ Jesus and I am more than a conqueror. Christ has already overcome this struggle for me. And I will be of good cheer. A better opportunity is on the way. I press on toward the goal for the prize of the upward call of God in Christ Jesus. (Philippians 3:14)

Chapter 2: Second Hand Stress Kills

Some people don't necessarily mean you any harm, but they don't do you any good either. It's called dead weight. Remove it.

Dealing With Other People's Stress

If I had to say anything about the subject of other people's stress, it would be this: it's not your responsibility. I know, we are our brother's keeper and many will disagree, but we are to be supportive and offer Godly council, not pick up the burden and carry it as if it were our own. We should give our stress and burdens to the Lord, not each other.

The effects of stress can be emotional. And it's hard enough for us to manage our own stress but when you have someone in your life who can't handle theirs, and they continually lean on you (or to put it more honestly - mire you down in their stressed-out world), it can be equally harmful and toxic. I'm talking beyond the occasional "shoulder to cry on". I mean, for instance, if you see them coming and you pray, *"Dear God, I really don't want to hear about xyz today!"* you're probably experiencing second hand stress.

If you are super empathetic like me, you may find yourself lying awake at night thinking about someone else's problems. The best thing to do pray for them.

Offer support and resources if you are blessed to do so. But don't take on so much that you become an emotional wreck. There are boundaries, well, there should be, when it comes to helping others. Boundaries are healthy.

Second-hand stress can affect you the same way your own stress does. I remember I was okay when I talked to my friend about her problems the first few times because, in small doses, it's very manageable. But when I was constantly exposed to her stressed out conversation, it became overwhelming. I started feeling tired after we talked. You see stress takes a toll on your physical body and your mental state. You might even be able to recognize the stress the moment you are around a certain person because your body reacts to their presence. Maybe your shoulder tenses or your head aches. Its because your body has become conditioned to respond to them.

Depression and anxiety might be the first thing you feel when you get around this person. Their tale is always one of chaos and frustration, never peace and calm. It can make you nervous talking to them.

When you're not in their presence you may find that you feel angry more often. This is especially true if the situation they've been sharing with you is something that causes you to become angry, too. They're drama has slowly seeped into your emotions and now their crisis has suddenly become your crisis.

Physically, your body will be slammed every time you come in contact with this person. Your blood pressure may even rise when you're in a conversation with this person. This may be normal depending on the topic of conversation, but if you already suffer from blood pressure issues, it can be disastrous for you to try juggling that person's stress load plus your own challenges. You're praying and trying to stay in faith about your issues. But they aren't. And you find yourself losing faith about your own circumstances because you're being infected by their negative emotions. *"Do not be deceived: Bad company ruins good morals. (1 Corinthians 15:33)*

Did you know that diabetes and heart disease are often associated with stress levels? And if you already have challenges with either one of these conditions, then being around stressed out people can be harmful to your health. Your prayers for healing are being compromised by the negativity that is infiltrating your soul. Everyone experiences stress but when you surround yourself with high-stressed emotionally-uncontrolled individuals, you're overdosing and it won't be healthy for you.

I recently heard another term "contagious stress". I think that's another good way to describe when others can project or pass their negative stress on to you. Contagious stress isn't stemming from your own life, but from someone else's. Because the stressed out person is in your life, you catch it easily, and many times, you become just as stressed.

A co-worker was having marital problems. Every day, she came to work stressed. She could hardly discuss her situation without beginning to cry. At first, I was very attentive and supportive. But somewhere between the third and fourth week of being around her, I began to feel drained. After work, I was exhausted and could hardly help my son with his homework. I noticed that I was becoming angry about things that hadn't bothered me before, like the neighbor's dog barking or my son forgetting to take out the garbage.

Some people don't know any better. And really need your prayers. But other folks purposely, like leeches, drain the life from you. Not only do they come to you to soothe their frustrations, but they also use you and feed off of you to get them through their tough times. Unfortunately, by doing this, they can drain you of your own good mood and faithful attitude. As a result, when something stressful happens to you in your own life, you may have trouble handling your emotions well because you're depleted of any positivity, thanks to their visit. Not only will their foul moods sway you to becoming more negative about life in general, but your new disposition also has a domino effect. You'll spread negativity to your spouse, your kids, your family, co-workers, and others. Now not only have you been contaminated, you're spreading the disease of negativity.

Types Of Second Hand Stress Relationships

Of course, we can't just ignore every stressing person in our lives. Some of those contagious people are part of our family and there's not getting rid of some of them. As the saying goes, "Families are like fudge — mostly sweet with a few nuts". As guardians, parents, and caregivers, our children's stress is our responsibility. If the young person in your life is enduring a lot of stress, with friends, schoolwork, sports, etc., then you need to shoulder the burden and help them get through the situation. But even then, there is an opportunity to teach them how to positively handle their emotions. By keeping cool and staying calm, we show them that there is a better way to handle stressful moments.

Married couples know the pressures of financial stress can cause emotions to flare. When our spouse is suffering, that's the time to control our own emotions and work together to figure out a solution. Whether it be a career crisis or not bringing in enough money, we can help them find ways to make positive changes. Remaining positive is key, not allowing emotions of fear or anxiety cause discord.

Still, though your ability to help is limited, especially if your loved one is continually miserable and complaining day after day without ever taking steps to remedy the situation, be patient. Pray for compassion and try to see the situation in a different light. You are not fighting against your child or spouse but rather, you are warring against strongholds, negative thought patterns, and stress.

For we wrestle not against flesh and blood, but against principalities, against powers, against the rulers of the darkness of this world, against spiritual wickedness in high places. Ephesians 6:12

Find out if the person wants or needs your input. If you're just a sounding board, and it never ends, then you'll have to use one of the methods listed later in this guide to help you find relief. Relationship stress is sometimes at the root of someone's unhappiness. A friend might confide in you about their life behind closed doors. If they're in danger, use your judgment and consider seeking help for them. I know this is touchy.

Once I was extremely stressed because I suspected a friend was being physically abused by her husband. She wouldn't admit to it. She claimed she was clumsy. I felt like she was brainwashed. I felt like he was a coward. I knew I couldn't share my emotions with her. It would only alienate her. I kept my calm and told her I'd always be there whenever she needed me. I did tell her that if I felt her life was ever in danger, I would call the police, with or without her permission. I gave her resources for shelters and encouraged her to get out. None of us are here to be doormats or punching bags. Abuse is one of those subjects that really pushes my buttons. I hate bullies. I hate people who prey on others. I had to step back emotionally. If I didn't control my own thoughts and actions, I would be no good for her when she needed me. I didn't want him to know how I felt either. I didn't want to chance him influencing her not to speak to me anymore. She needed a positive safe environment and I had to keep my calm so that I could offer that support when she was ready. I also had to pray for wisdom and peace while being there for her.

> **"I shall stay calm in moments of stress and anxiety, so as to allow positive thoughts and actions to manifest from me." Len Brown**

Money stress is common for many people. Some friends or family might just be venting and sharing, whereas others are telling you in an effort to get you to bail them out of a money mess. I've been in both situations and both can be stressful. In the first case, of venting, I listened. But I'm a strong believer that I should help where I can. For instance, one of my aunt's was venting about her bills and how purchasing propane for the winter was going to be a burden. So I offered (insisted) help. Use your best judgment. I also had an acquaintance who constantly got into money binds because of poor spending habits. I'm not judging here. This person would purchase an expensive pair of shoes instead of paying their utility bill and then call around for people to bail them out. I admit I did help the first couple of times.

Health stress is one situation where you can help a friend or loved one shoulder the burden. If a friend needs to talk about their battle with cancer, for instance, then it's helpful if you're there for them, even offering to run errands or go to appointments with them. To help you deal with this stress, you can practice stress-relieving measures yourself. We pray always, but there are other things I do to relax like, hot baths, aromatherapy, or exercising.

With health stress, if it's short term, it probably won't be an issue. But if you know someone dealing with long-term, or terminal illness, be careful to stay calm and not allow yourself to become overwhelmed. Ask God to help you be the calm in the midst of their storm. When my aunt was going through her illness, she had certain people she enjoyed being around because she said we calmed her spirit. It was tough, but God was there every step of the way. That's what we, as believers, should do for each other. We should calm each other's spirits. But we can only do so when our own spirits are calm and Christ-centered.

> ***Being positive in a negative situation is not naïve, its leadership.-Unknown***

You have to gauge which type of stress your friend or family member is presenting. Is it something where you should be there for them unconditionally, or is it a situation where you're exposing yourself to someone who refuses to take responsibility and merely wants another person to feel the pain with them? I know it's difficult, but you have to take your emotional health into consideration. You can't help anyone if you're out of control yourself. Remember, just because someone is complaining to you or sharing their problems, it doesn't mean that they necessarily want to take steps to improve their situation.

> **"Some people don't necessarily mean you any harm but they don't do you any good either...it's called dead weight. Remove it."**

Skip the pity parties. It's okay, go ahead and un-invite yourself! Chronic complainers don't really want help or solutions. They really just want you to be there to listen and witness their emotional meltdown. You don't have to, so if you can avoid doing so, by all means, get away.

Health Issues Caused By Stress

> *I do not fix problems. I fix my thinking. Then problems fix themselves.-Louis Hay*

Let's talk about the health issues a bit. I believe our health truly is our wealth. And the enemy knows that so he tries to stress us out to the point of no return. He wants us to be sick and unhealthy. He wants us to die and not witness the Gospel. So let's not be ignorant of his devices. Let's be wise about our health and the effects of stress and the impact of constant emotional turmoil.

Studies show that older adults, women in general, especially working mothers and pregnant women, less-educated people, divorced or widowed people, people experiencing financial strains such as long-term unemployment, people who are the targets of discrimination, uninsured and underinsured people, and people who simply live in cities all seem to be particularly susceptible to health-related stress problems.

Here's an excerpt from an interesting piece I read online:

...individuals can take up to a year to recover a healthy immune system following the death of their spouse, and long-term caregivers have suppressed immune systems compared with persons in the general population. Studies on survivors of sexual abuse and those with post-traumatic stress disorder suggest they have elevated levels of stress hormones, as do students at exam time. In these groups of people and others experiencing loneliness, anger, trauma and relationship problems, infections last longer and wounds take longer to heal.

However, having fun with friends and family seems to have the opposite effect on our immune systems. Social contact and laughter have a measurable effect for several hours. Relaxation through massage or listening to music also reduces stress hormones.

***How Does Mood Effect Immunity*, by Jane Collingwood** (*http://psychcentral.com*)

Isn't that something? When our mood is poor, we are not just "in a bad mood". We are in an unhealthy mood. We are negativity impacting our health. And, in essence, we are tearing down our temple (1Cor. 6:19-20)

Ms. Collingwood also says in her article that stress results in increased risk of arthritis and multiple sclerosis. And can worsen skin conditions like psoriasis, eczema, hives, and acne. What's worse, stress can also trigger asthma attacks. I've personally experienced the worsening of acne and asthma attacks brought on by stress.

Additionally, our emotional health influences how we perceive what is happening to us. People who are less emotionally stable or have high anxiety levels tend to experience certain events as more stressful than healthy people do. And the lack of an established network of family and friends predisposes us to stress-related health problems such as heart disease and infections. Caregivers, children, and medical professionals are also frequently found to be at higher risk for stress-related disorders.

Job-related stress is particularly likely to be chronic because it is such a large part of life. Stress reduces a worker's effectiveness by impairing concentration, causing sleeplessness and increasing the risk of illness, back problems, accidents, and lost time. At its worst extremes, stress that places a burden on our hearts and circulation can often be fatal.

A stress-filled life really seems to raise the odds of heart disease and stroke down the road. Researchers have found that after middle-age, those who report chronic stress face a somewhat higher risk of fatal or non-fatal heart disease or stroke over the years. It is now believed that constant stress takes its toll on our arteries, causing chronically high levels of stress hormones and pushing people to maintain unhealthy habits like smoking.

Simply put, too much stress puts you at dire risk for health problems. Whether it comes from one event or the buildup of many small events, stress causes major physical alterations that often lead to health problems. Here is a list of some of these changes:
Stress is always with us controlling what we do and how we feel. If you're stressed, you do things faster and in an unhappier way. Although you don't want to

overreact to stress, you don't want to just hide your stress either. Ignoring your stress will only eat at you, hurting your emotions and your relationships. By being aggressive toward another person, you temporarily feel relief, but then reality kicks in as you feel more stressed from hurting the other person.

We need to learn ways to manage our stress and not let it get the better of us and the people we see daily. Stress can motivate us to take action and get our behinds in gear. But, too often, stress works against us. That's why we must manage it effectively. Here are a few Do's and Don'ts:

1) Don't worry – Worrying is extremely dangerous for your health. By worrying, you increase the chances of having a heart-attack and you become miserable.
2) Don't beat yourself up or stress over, "What if…" or "What might happen…" Stop trying to predict the future. You cannot control everything. Ask God for help with what is in your control and give the rest over to Him.
3) Don't involve too many people – If someone isn't involved, just leave them out of the situation. Things will only become worse when they start throwing their emotions into the mix as well. It is so tempting to

release your stress on other people. But remember, not everyone can handle your problem. They may become more stressed than you and they may even try to solve the problem or act on your behalf. I've seen this happen when couples fight and involve others. Family and friends become upset and take matters into their own hands, causing the stress to increase for everyone involved. If you must, limit yourself to one or two level-headed people only.

4) Do Take Responsibility – When you take responsibility, you live in truth. You do not become a victim of others. You begin to control and create your feelings. You stop blaming others for what has happened to you and you become proactive controlling thoughts, feelings, and stresses. By accepting responsibility as way of managing stress, you begin self-control.

5) Do Use Self-control – You are in complete control of your emotions. It's by learning to manage your mind that you correctly manage your stress. No matter how badly you want to "go off" on someone, don't. It will only stress you out more in the long run. There is always a chance that you will have to face this person again. You don't want to do anything to hurt someone else. Remember, you have complete control of your

emotions and actions. However, your ability to be in control of your emotions and actions is dependent on your desire and discipline to do so.

6) Do Be Self-Aware – You need to manage yourself and control your emotions. You need to be aware if you are treating a person in an appropriate way because of the stress. You need to know that you are stressed, why you are stressed, and ways to manage the stress.

7) Do Push Forward –Winston Churchill said, "If you are going through hell, keep going." Don't stop and give up. I encourage you to stop, relax, and be smart, but do not lose the perseverance to keep going. If you are going through a bad patch in life, by stopping there, you remain in the bad patch. Don't get stuck. Keep it moving.

8) Do Go on a Retreat –If you can afford a holiday, go for it! For those who can't do that, take a stay-cation, stay home turn off phones and social media and just recharge. Take long walks or work out. You may just need to go away for a bit to refresh your mind. By being active, you release hormones that counteract stress.

Stress can make us miserable if it is not managed. Learn these ways to manage your stress, and you'll have stress working for you and not you for it.

Vitamins and Minerals and Stress, Oh My!

Medical research has proved that during stressful situations, particular vitamins are needed to maintain proper functioning nervous and endocrine systems.

Deficiencies of vitamins B-1, B-5, and B-6, can lead to anxiety reactions, depression, insomnia, and cardiovascular weaknesses, while vitamins B-2 and niacin deficiencies have been known to cause stomach irritability and muscular weakness. Their depletion lowers your tolerance to and ability to cope with stressors.

One widely popular theory is that the body's need for vitamin C increases when under stress. Vitamin C is stored in the adrenal gland. After the gland releases adrenal hormones as part of the stress response, the supply needs to be replenished. The production of adrenal hormones is accelerated by vitamin C. Vitamin C is also needed for the synthesis of the thyroid hormone. Thyroid hormone production regulates the body's metabolism. Thus, when the metabolic rate increases under stress, so does the need for vitamin C.

Stress management is a lifelong process. With a successful stress management program, you'll note positive changes in your health, well-being, relationships, and overall performance.

Don't let the enemy use stress to destroy you and the people you love. Control your emotions and manage your stress. Remember: "No temptation has overtaken you except what is common to mankind. And God is faithful; he will not let you be tempted beyond what you can bear. But when you are tempted, he will also provide a way out so that you can endure it." (1Corinthians 10:13). You can do it!

Chapter 3: Deliver Me From Misery Loves Company

We talked about contagious people earlier, but let's talk a bit more about the purposely miserable people. Instead of being inspired by your positive outlook and using it to improve their own lives, **Misery Loves Company** prefers to drag you down with them. You know, "Misery loves company." They want to not feel so alone, and if you allow them to, they'll chain you to their problems, which isn't healthy for either of you. Luckily, there are a couple of simple things you can do to minimize stress they bring on. There are some people who you have to (or want to) continue being around. For these individuals, we need to have a plan in place where you can manage their stress so that it's not affecting you. This is a situation where you know ahead of time what you're getting into, and yet you're able to prevent their troubles from infecting your own life. There are three ways you can achieve this.

First, try steering conversations away from the repeat stress topics. For example, let's say your coworker is also a good friend but continually gripes about their spouse every time you are around them. I've had this happen to me and it's not fun. It reached the point I was exhausted hearing about it and I began avoiding this person completely. What could have been a great friendship eventually fizzled out because I just couldn't take it. I have a real issue with people who continually complain but never take steps to make changes.

The best thing to do is acknowledge what they say, offer condolences that they're going through that, and then perk the conversion up to something more positive. For example:

Friend: "Robert really gets on my nerves. He never spends time with me anymore. All he does is hang out on those stupid social media sites day and night."

You: "I understand that must hurt your feelings. Hey! Why don't we go shopping next weekend? Have you been to the new outlet across town? There are some great deals!"

By acknowledging, you let them know that you were listening. You showed that you cared by offering condolences. But instead of hopping down the emotional bunny trail with them, you offered a positive spin on the situation. If they try to drag you back into the conversation, just nod, and say, "I'm sorry." and change the topic again. I do this all the time. It's better than zoning out on them completely or allowing them to dump their negative emotions on you.

Try not to ask questions or be a relationship counselor, you'll soon find out that you aren't qualified to deal with their issue or they will blow you off completely and continue ranting. This will only frustrate you. If you want, get the business card of a relationship counselor and say something like, "I remembered our talk. I thought about you and picked this up the other day as I'm not equipped to help you deal with it, so I hope this helps!" and then change the subject to a more positive topic.

The second thing you can do is build yourself up in faith. Shield your heart and mind by praying and reading scripture before you see them. Ephesians 6:11 warns us, *"Put on the whole armor of God, that you may be able to stand against the schemes of the devil."* If you're able to do this, your friend can mutter on and on about their woes and you'll be just fine nodding your head, sympathizing, and never let it invade your emotional well-being. While they're going on and on about how miserable they are, you're thinking of the scriptures like Philippians 4:8-9:

"Finally, brethren, whatsoever things are true, whatsoever things are honest, whatsoever things are just, whatsoever things are pure, whatsoever things are lovely, whatsoever things are of good report; if there be any virtue, and if there be any praise, think on these things....and the peace of God shall be with you."

This can take a little practice, but I'm telling you it works. Once you get it down, you will be able to let what they are saying go in one ear and out the other. I know it sounds rude. But, it's not. It's self-preservation, more than anything. You're consciously putting up a barriers so their negative emotions aren't absorbed into your soul.

You know the negativity has penetrated if, after having contact with family either by phone or in person, you become depressed, argumentative, self-critical, perfectionistic, angry, combative, or withdrawn. It's as if you've been contaminated with negativity.

Sometimes, when you're unable to distance yourself in one way (like becoming emotionally un-invested in their issues), you have to distance yourself a different way - physically.

A third option for escaping other people's drama is to walk away. It doesn't mean you have to cut all ties. (Although, in extreme cases, that may be what has to happen, depending on how bad it's affecting you and your family).

> **"As for a person who stirs up division, after warning him once and then twice, have nothing more to do with him," Titus 3:10**

Set a limit on your phone conversations. If your friend has a habit of calling you after work and droning on and on for two hours about their horrible life, make it a point to end the conversation at a certain amount of time, like 15-20 minutes. In fact, you might tell the person when they first call that you can't talk long. Meet with them in settings where other people or distractions are present. These kinds of stressed people usually want all of the attention on themselves. They don't want to share the spotlight, so by forcing it to be in a place where your attention is divided, they'll feel less like sharing - or if they do, you'll easily be able to get out of the conversation and seek relief.

> **"I urge you, brothers and sisters, to watch out for those who cause divisions and put obstacles in your way that are contrary to the teaching you have learned. Keep away from them."**
> **Romans 16:17**

Be honest with them about how their stress is affecting your life. Some people just aren't aware of how they act. In a loving way, let them know that you care about them and sympathize with their situation - but you have to alleviate stress in your life for your own reasons, so you'll need to keep the conversation light. Now what **true** friend wouldn't understand that?

It's okay to set these boundaries. They are needed if you are going to win the battle of controlling your emotions and not allowing outside influences to take you on an emotional roller coaster ride.

Deliver Me From The Enemy

Let's not forget that we have an adversary, the Devil, the originator of **Misery Loves Company**. He is the most miserable soul of all. He's so miserable that he has made it his mission to make as many of us miserable, angry, depressed, and oppressed as he possible can when we are here on earth. We've talked a lot about the people in our lives and how their negative emotions can influence ours, but we always have to remember that it's possible that they are being negatively influenced by the enemy.

Keep them in prayer. Pray for yourself and your family daily that you do no fall prey to the negative influences of the enemy. The depression, anger, guilt that weighs you down is not from the Father above. If you have any emotions that are uncontrolled, violent, or hurtful, don't just ignore them. Pray for help and guidance. Ask God to help you address them. He loves you dearly and wants you to live a joyful and peaceful life.

For we wrestle not against flesh and blood, but against principalities, against powers, against the rulers of the darkness of this world, against spiritual wickedness in high places. —*Ephesians 6:12*

Chapter 4: Emotion Control: A Look At Anger

Anger is an emotion that makes your mouth act quicker than your brain. Take a deep breath and think before you speak.

I mentioned anger earlier. And how I use anger emotions to motivate me. Let's talk more. It takes two people to have an argument and it's often the case that each person "fuels" the anger and the emotions in the other by extending and aggravating the tone of the conversation. As the situation continues like this, it is more likely to end up in a confrontation and generate a bad ending.

It's important to exercise emotional control and to be able to control the messages that you send to your brain, to reduce the likelihood of an emotionally charged reaction. Always try and avoid extreme reactions to any situation.

Anger is a real problem in today's society. Just watch the evening news and you're bound to see a story about someone losing their cool at work, school, or even the local department store. For this reason, it is important that we learn how to cope with anger issues. As believers, we want to be part of the solution, not the problem.

Everyone, at some time or another in their lives, has experienced anger and perhaps even lashed out in anger. I always marvel at Jesus' display of anger in the temple. The thought of Jesus becoming so upset that he flipped over tables, just astounds me. (Matthew 21:12) *Did He lose control? What was He thinking? Did He feel regret afterward?* I'm going to ask Him when I meet Him. But I digress. So….If Jesus became so angry that he did something like that, what does that mean for little old us? Can we truly control our anger?

"Be ye angry, and sin not: let not the sun go down upon your wrath." *Ephesians 4:26*

Anger is a natural emotion, because we all become hurt, aggravated, insulted, or feel threatened from time to time. Anger can be your greatest ally or your greatest foe. For example, if we feel threatened by another person and we express our anger in a controlled way, the outcome can be favorable. Conversely, if we become out of control, the situation can escalate and become worse than it was before.

NEGATIVE EMOTION + NEGATIVE MEDITATION = NEGATION REACTION
NEGATIVE EMOTON +POSITIVE MEDITATION=HEALTHY EMOTIONAL RESPONSE

When we control our thoughts that lead to our emotions, we benefit tremendously. Our emotions become healthy responses. They protect us and warn us of imminent danger. They tell us when something needs to change. And they help us handle crisis situations. However, if we allow our anger to get the better of us, we put our well-being, our health, and, sometimes, even others at risk.

> **But the fruit of the Spirit is love, joy, peace, patience, kindness, goodness, faithfulness, gentleness, self-control; against such things there is no law. Galatians 5:22-23**

I remember feeling terrified as I witnessed a family member allow her anger to get the best of her. Someone was threatening her child and she reacted in such a way that I'd never seen. It was as if she wasn't herself anymore. She was yelling and cursing. Then, she abruptly hung up, dashed to her gun case and took out a pistol. Shocked and scared, I tried to talk her out of leaving. But she sped off in her car determined to "set them straight". Thankfully, no one was hurt. By the time she reached her destination, she'd decided to leave the gun in the car. The situation did become pretty heated, but there was no violence or use of weapons.

It is not uncommon for someone to ignore the problem in dealing with anger. The person might be in denial of any negative behavior he or she has exhibited. Denial is a big reason why some people never deal with their problems, or their anger.

"Anger is a sign that something needs to change." Mark Epstein

I know that a person can only take so much before they blow their top at some point. And we all have a boiling point. Some of us have higher capacity to handle stressful triggers than others. Part of the problem is, somewhere down the line, we weren't given the tools to deal with our emotions effectively. I know, growing up, it wasn't something that we discussed. In my family, we simply suppressed our emotions. As a result, there are some of us now, as adults, who have serious anger issues (don't tell them I said that-smile).

Uncontrolled emotions are complicated and damaging. They can sap the life from a person. Therefore, when we know how to cope with our feelings and emotions, we are on a path to success. Nothing is more gratifying than feeling a sense of control. It's a personal achievement that is vital to our emotional well-being and our spiritual walk.

Surrounding yourself with positive people is so crucial. When we surround ourselves with positive people, we will pick up their positive habits. But if we are spending time with hot-heads, chances are, we will be influenced by their negative attitude. And when trouble comes, we are more likely to lose control.

Have you ever had an emotional outburst? Do you remember how you felt immediately following? You probably remember feeling disappointment, frustration, embarrassment, and maybe even sadness. Losing control is not very pleasant and, deep down within ourselves, we know that it's simply "not right." The feeling you get in the moment immediately following the outburst is your indication. I have read about people who have no remorse, conscience, or moral compass, but those people have a personality disorder. If you don't have a personality disorder or illness and your anger is out of control, simply put, you need help.

As peacekeepers, we have a responsibility to practice anger control. If you're having trouble in this area, here are a few tried and true ways to diffuse and or manage your anger:

Counting To 10 Actually Does Help. You have probably heard people advise you that you should count from 1 to 10 whenever you begin to feel angry. As crazy as this sounds and as difficult as it might be to do whenever those emotional feelings are welling up inside you, it's amazing what can happen if you physically do employ this tactic. It absolutely can help to diffuse your temper.

Stop Engaging And Walk Away. In our crazy, stereotyped society, it might be seen as weak to actually turn and walk away from an emotive situation. Doing so, however, will almost invariably diffuse the situation and the person who initiates this movement is ultimately the stronger of the two. This is one of the best ways of controlling anger, but it's not to say that you should let those emotions bottle up inside you, either. You do need to address the situation that's causing the disagreement or confrontation, but must do it in a controlled and non-confrontational way. If you let it stew up inside, that's not healthy either.

Often, anger management control is rooted in an ability to be rational and to be able to identify solutions to any problem or situation. If you can come up with a solution that will include, if necessary, the ability to "own" the problem, then you will already be looking at this from a positive angle.

Consider Other Perspectives. Sometimes, your anger may well be justified but you have to deal with it in a calm way. When you can feel the emotion of anger beginning to bubble over, you have to be able to look at the situation from every possible anger, not just your own point of view. Any attempt at a confrontational approach will likely initiate angry defensive mechanisms in everyone involved.

Do Something Constructive. When I begin to feel myself becoming angry, I do something productive. My favorite thing to do is cleaning. The chores need to be done anyway and by the time I'm done, I've calmed down, the cleaning is done, and I feel better. Another thing I do is workout. I plop in a workout dvd or lace up my sneakers and head to the park or local track.

Stop And Smell The Blessings. Okay, the saying is "smell the roses" but in this case, try counting your blessings. Think of the good things that are happening in your life. Think of something that you have to be grateful for. Remember "…think on these things and the peace of God will be with you." (Philippians 4:8)

Anxiety Attacks

You will keep him in perfect peace, whose mind is stayed on you, because he trusts in you. (Isaiah 26:3)
The first time I had an anxiety attack, I had no idea what was happening. I was driving home, thinking about my marriage and contemplating divorce. My then husband and I had gotten into a terrible argument and we'd decided to separate. I remember, out of nowhere, I began feeling like I couldn't breathe. I was taking deep breaths but it wasn't working. I let the windows down and inhaled the evening air. It seemed to help. And remember thinking, "This is stress and I have to let it go." The rest of the drive home, I tried to focus on other things, my son, my nieces and nephews, anything that made me happy. By the time I made it home, I was breathing normally. That experience taught me that stress can, and will, trigger anxiety.

Anyone who has ever suffered the horror of a panic attack knows that they are real, even if they are very difficult to quantify or describe. Sometimes, these attacks can last for minutes on end, which, in turn, feel more like hours. It's important to be able to get to the bottom of any triggers and to try and make changes to your life accordingly.

If you want to know how to stop anxiety, then you have to understand why you are anxious. You might think that the answer to that question is rather easy to come up with, as the majority of us face so much on any given day that an elevated level of anxiety is simply understandable.

You may have money issues, job worries, health concerns, or all three at the same time. If you have a lot of time on your hands, then you may have a tendency to sit and reflect too much on the wrong things, all of which can help to contribute to the feeling of anxiety. If you find that an attack seems to come out of the blue, ask yourself exactly what you were doing immediately before. There are almost always triggers, but they may not be as obvious. Remember that certain stimulants, such as those that are found in coffee, energy drinks, and cigarettes can be to blame. If you haven't been eating properly or sleeping as well as you should, you might be creating a bad environment in this way.

These episodes can be really disturbing and frightening. I know mine was. When you feel one coming on, you want to know how to stop anxiety attack repercussions before they get out of hand. However, sometimes, it can feel that merely focusing on the fact that you might be having an attack can make it worse. Some people suggest breathing into a paper bag. I'm not sure if this really works. I know that it at least makes you to slow down and focus on your breathing. (Inhaling slowly through the nose, before exhaling steadily and slowly through the mouth). This can, in turn, help to slow down your heart rate and fend off the attack itself.

If life seems overwhelming, try to remember this prayer: "God, *grant me the serenity* to accept the things I cannot change; courage to change the things I can; and wisdom to know the difference." Take one day at a time. By focusing only on one issue before you move on to the next, you can start to make sense of it all. When your racing thoughts just accumulate everything together until it becomes one big problem, it can all seem to be insurmountable. The problem begins to magnify.

Don't be afraid to evaluate your thoughts and emotions to find the potential causes of the attacks. In other words, don't just bury your pain. Deal with it. But deal with it knowing that you have the power of God backing you. By figuring out what's causing the attacks, you won't invariably bring on one of the attacks, but you will be able to identify some of the steps you can take to help avoid them in the future. Take one step at a time, dealing with and hopefully eliminating the potential triggers. If money problems are a trigger, find out what God says about your finances. *2 Corinthians 9:8* says: "*And God is able to make all grace abound toward you; that ye, always having all sufficiency in all things, may abound to every good work." Whenever we need money or possessions, prayer is the answer. Look to the Lord, because He will provide it-according to His will.*

Meditate on His word and clear your mind of doubt. Praise God for His goodness. Put on some worship Music and worship your provider. Offer a sacrifice of praise (Hebrews 13:15). I know from experience that anxiety will flee when you emerge yourself in praise and worship. The Lord inhabits the praises of His people (Psalm 22:3). And when God comes in Anxiety runs out kicking and screaming!

Depressed Thoughts

God said don't look around because you'll be impressed. Don't look down you'll be depressed; just look to me and you'll be blessed.-unknown

When my 46 year old mother died suddenly of a pulmonary embolism, I went into a depression. I didn't want to get out of bed. I didn't want to pray. I didn't want to do anything but lay in bed and cry. I felt like I was surrounded by an invisible barrier. I was in a bubble. And the last thing I wanted to do was "talk about it". Depression can manifest itself in many different ways. You might have a feeling of hopelessness, which can lead to withdrawal, inactivity, and a complete lack of productivity.

You might feel as if you're not able to concentrate at all and just can't get down to work as you used to. You might also feel as if you're tired, have no motivation or energy whatsoever, yet have considerable difficulty sleeping. Do you lie awake in bed for hours on end, only to find that when you do get to sleep you have difficulty waking up and listening to that alarm bell? Depression is a very serious matter, which does not discriminate. Depression does not care what your age is, what gender you are, or even what your race or social class is. Depression can often make a person feel sad, helpless, hopeless, and irritable. It is normal for people to have these feeling sometimes, but some people cannot just snap out of it and this is the difference between what is normal and major depression. It is the determination and brutality of the emotions that determine the mental illness of depression from normal mood changes.

A Prayer Against Depression

God, I have been carrying a heavy burden and I am coming to You right now for relief. I surrender all my hurts, disappointments, and insecurities to You. Thank You for Your Word, which tells me about Your unconditional love and affection for me. You are my

Father, and I am Your child. I love to be in Your presence, You are the source of all my peace and joy. Forever I will praise You. Amen.- Joyce Meyer

Depression is an illness that affects your body, mind, disposition, thought, sleep, energy, concentration, weight, and much more. Depression is not a mood, and it is not a sign of personal weakness. Clinical depression is constant and can interfere significantly with an individual's ability to function by emotional experiences of sadness, loss, or passing mood states. If you are depressed, don't ignore it, but don't give in to it either. Clinical depression can be devastating to all areas of a person's everyday life, including family relationships, friendships, and the ability to work or go to school.

I want to mention another type of illness that involves depression. That is Bipolar disorder (manic-depression), a mood disorder or abnormalities of mood. Bipolar disorder involves episodes of both serious mania and depression. Bipolar disorder, like clinical depression, can have a devastating impact on sufferer's life if it is not treated. I've witnessed untreated Bipolar disorder and it's very frightening, especially if it's someone you care for deeply. Acknowledging that there is a problem and getting help is so important.

Major depression is a more common illness, the symptoms of which are mainly those of 'low' mood. Someone close to me had major depression and it lead to his complete breakdown. He finally accepted that he needed help and he saw a doctor. Today, he is living much healthier and happier and his family reunited and happy.

If you're feel low constantly, you don't want to get out bed, easily frustrated, and feeling sick all the time, you may be experiencing depression. The immune system of a depressed person is usually very low and, therefore, ineffectively responding to diseases, including cancer. It's important that you deal with it immediately, not just for you but for the people you love. They are suffering, too.

When you are feeling depressed, you tend to push other people away from you and it's unfortunate that many people are not able to recognize the symptoms of depression in others, or to be sympathetic. As we are all supposed to be "tough" in this society, people have a tendency to tell you to "snap out of it", or something similarly unhelpful.

"Mental pain is less dramatic than physical pain, but it is more common and also more hard to bear.

The frequent attempt to conceal mental pain increases the burden: it is easier to say "My tooth is

aching" than to say "My heart is broken."

— **C.S. Lewis,** *The Problem of Pain*

If you have been feeling depressed for a long period of time, but are unable to explain why or know what to do about it, you need to take action. Sometimes, you need significant lifestyle changes. If you have a tendency to drink too much or use other drugs, this is almost certainly contributory. If you have a lot of time on your hands then you can often let your racing, and maybe negative, thoughts take over. Lifestyle changes can help to make a difference.

We are not what happens to us, who we get to be is who we say we're going to be in the world-Gary of ProjectForgive.com

All of us will feel depressed at one moment or another but for many, like myself, thankfully, these feelings dissipate and go away. However, in quite a significant number of people, depression can be difficult to deal with and even life altering. And triggers such as relationship ending, a death in the family, or loss of a job can have a devastating impact. If you're feeling depressed or down, there are some simple steps you can take on your own to start improving your mood:

**Start your day with an inspirational quote or scripture reading.

**Have a good look at what you eat. Are you getting the right amount of vitamins, nutrients and minerals? Many advocate a diet that is rich in vegetables and fruit and has a good amount of omega-3 fatty acids.

**Get out and about as much as you can and soak in some of the warm sunlight, within reason, of course.

**Take up a new hobby or pastime and is definitely the time to seek out people who are invariably happy, positive, and upbeat.

**Dedicate time to prayer and meditation. Use a simple <u>inspirational devotional</u> or read passages from your Bible.

Never be afraid to reach out to wise counsel, specialist, or medical professionals if you think that you cannot cope any longer with this depression. Recognize self-destructive behavior, especially over reliance on alcohol as a prime example and seek help, if necessary, to control this, too.

Depression is definitely treatable, whether through prescription drugs, alternative medicine, counseling, lifestyle changes, or a combination of all of these. You don't have to suffer through it, needlessly. For *God has not given us* a spirit of fear, but of power and of love and of a sound mind. (2 Timothy 1:7)

Peace.

It does not mean to be in a place where there is no noise, trouble, or hard work, it means to be in the midst of those things and still be calm in your heart.-unknown

Chapter 5: Finding True Happiness

"I let go. I accept my life as it is. I do not judge. I do not dramatize. I let life's events come freely and I welcome the lessons they convey. I stop struggling now. I let go and know that God always gives me that which is most appropriate for my soul."

Almost everyone have heard the hit single, *Don't Worry, Be Happy* by Bobby McFerrin. The song has a very catchy way of conveying its message of being happy to everyone. Bobby McFerrin's simple message surely made a lot of people by telling them not to worry.

"Come to me, all you who are weary and burdened, and I will give you rest. Take my yoke upon you and learn from me, for I am gentle and humble in heart, and you will find rest for your souls. For my yoke is easy and my burden is light." (Matthew 11: 28-30)

We've already covered the health risks of stress. So by now, you know that stress brought on by constant worrying is linked to top causes of death such as heart disease, cancer, and stroke. These reasons alone should encourage us to live a stress-free life.

There may be a tiny percentage of people who want to be miserable. But for the most part, I believe we all want to live a happy, resilient, and optimistic life. Being happy is "characterized by characterized by or indicative of pleasure, contentment, or joy."

I believe the key words in that definition are contentment and joy. There are two scriptures dealing with these subjects that I live by and I think they will be a blessing to you as well.

**"Not that I speak in respect of want: for I have learned, in *whatsoever state I am*, therewith to be *content*." (Philippians 4:11)

**"Consider it pure joy, my brothers and sisters, whenever you face trials of many kinds, because you know that the testing of your faith produces perseverance." – James 1:2-3 (NIV).

Being happy is not about your circumstances being absolutely perfect. It's about finding inner peace and joy in life, despite the trials and challenges. But how do you do that? You make up your mind that you are going to trust beyond yourself. That anything out of your control is still in God's control. Knowing that what you are experiencing will work to your advantage, somehow. And more importantly, you don't have to know how. It may hurt temporarily but it will not hurt forever. One day, you will wake up and everything will be okay.

Abraham Lincoln observed that most people, most of the time, can choose how happy or stressed, how relaxed or troubled, how bright or dull their outlook to be. "Folks are usually about as happy as they make their minds up to be." You see, in his mind, the choice is simple really, choose to be happy. Not because of an outside influence, but an internal choice.

Here are some ways to keep negative emotions at bay and achieve internal happiness:

**Be grateful. We have so much to be thankful for. Thank the waiter for bringing your food, the housekeeper for keeping your home, the babysitter for watching your kids. Also thank the carrier for delivering your packages, thank the policeman for making your place safe, and thank God for being alive.

**Watch the news less. It's stressful. Some people just can't start their day without their daily dose of news. Think about it, 99% of the news we hear or read is bad news. Starting the day with bad news does not seem to be a sensible thing to do.

**A spiritual connection is vital. Being part of a good church, Bible study, or other God-centered group with its singing, sacraments, prayers, and meditations can help foster inner peace.

**Manage your time. Time is invaluable and too important to waste. Time management can be viewed as a list of rules that involves scheduling, setting goals, planning, creating lists of things to do, and prioritizing.
**My favorite thing to do- Laugh! Laugh and Laugh heartily every day. Heard a good joke? Tell your friends or family about it. As they also say, *Laughter is the best medicine.* Psalm 126:2 says, "Then was our mouth filled with laughter, and our tongue with singing: then said they among the heathen, The LORD hath done great things for them."

**Try not to keep anger or frustration pent up, this is bad for your health. Instead, find ways of expressing them in a way that will not cause more injury or hurt to anyone. Express your feelings, affections, friendship, and passion to positive people around you. They will most likely reciprocate with words of encouragement and comfort that will inspire you.

**Finish a project. Hard work and completing a task

brings tremendous personal satisfaction. It gives a feeling of being competent and capable. During one my most difficult times, I redecorated my dining room. It turned out beautiful and really lifted my mood. As I sit in it typing today, it still makes me happy. Accomplishments are necessary for all of us, they give us a sense of value. Work on things that you feel worthy of your time.

**Another one of my favorites- Learn something new. Try and learn something new every day. Learning also makes us expand and broaden our horizons. And could also give us more opportunities in the future.

**I know I've said this in other chapters, but exercise is so good for your emotional health. Run, jog, walk, and do other things that your body was made for. Feel alive.
**Avoid exposure to negative elements like loud noises, toxins, and hazardous places.
And always remember the quote from Abraham Lincoln, he says that, "Most people are about as happy as they make up their minds to be."

Learning To Love Yourself

The second greatest commandment: *You shall love your neighbor as yourself.* **(Mark 12:31.)**

Love yourself. Accept yourself. Embrace your personality and yes, even your imperfect emotions. Know that Jesus died for you because He knew you had flaws. And He still wanted you to be reconciled with the Father so that you would have eternal life. You don't have to be perfect or get it all right today. As long as your heart is right before God and you are making progress, that's what counts.

How can we fulfill the command to love our neighbors, if we cannot love ourselves? We need to be filled with the unconditional love of a healing God, before we can forgive others or be healed of emotional challenges ourselves.

Be thankful and appreciate how God made you. Understand that if there is a problem with your emotions, your health, or your physical body, your Creator is ready and willing to help you. He loves you tremendously. Rejecting or hating yourself is not what God wants for you. Self-hatred is no more from God than uncontrolled emotions are. God is a God of love and order. "For *God* is not the author of confusion, but of peace," (1Corinthians 14:33)

"Whoever does not love does not know God, because ***God is love." (1 John 4:8)***

Thank God for creating you in His image. Accept that He says you are "fearfully and wonderfully made". You may not feel like it today. And you certainly may not feel like it when your emotions get the best of you. You are more than a mere physical body. You are more than your emotions. Inside you dwells a perfect spirit.

Psalms 139:14, "I will praise thee; for I am fearfully and wonderfully made: marvelous are thy works; and that my soul knoweth right well."

Get rid of the notion that you have to be perfect. Only God is perfect (Mark 10:18). His son, Jesus was crucified for your imperfections. Stop trying to crucify yourself. Christ paid it all. God loves you. And He wants you to see yourself the way that He sees you. As a marvelous creation.

I know you want a better life and you deserve one. You deserve peace. You can be free from destructive emotions and misery-loving people. The next time you feel like your emotions are trying to take control, stop yourself. If necessary walk away. Listen to the still small voice in your heart saying, "Peace be still". That voice is the Creator, the one who loves you beyond measure. Know that you are fearfully and wonderfully made. You don't have to act out to prove a point. Christ proved your point on the cross. Live the abundant life He died for you to experience. A life of order, peace, prosperity, and love. God bless.

Find Your Peace
"Ego says: Once everything falls into place, I'll find peace. Spirit says: find your peace, and then everything will fall into place." –Marianne Williamson

Chapter 6: Quotes About Emotions

Never reply when you are angry. Never make a promise when you are happy. Never make a decision when you are sad.

Some days you can't make heads or tails of life. These are the days to put stress aside and do what feels good to you. Tomorrow is a new day and things will make sense given time.-Anna Pereira

There are realities we all share, regardless of our nationality, language, or individual tastes. As we need food, so do we need emotional nourishment: love, kindness, appreciation, and support from others.-J. Donald Walters

Emotions are temporary states of mind, don't let them permanently destroy you.

Sometimes it's better to break down in tears and show some emotion than to keep it all inside and not tell a single soul.

Genius is the ability to renew one's emotions in daily experience. –Paul Cezanne

Any emotion is a weapon of huge power.

Even if you can't control your emotion, you can control your response.

The mind may never achieve or express anything great unless emotion plays a part. –Ben Johnson

Your intellect may be confused but your emotions will never lie to you.-Roger Ebert

Anger is an emotion that makes your mouth act quicker than your brain. Take a deep breath and think before you speak.

One who has control over their emotions has great power over those who don't!

Acting is not being emotional, but being able to express emotion.-Kate Reid

Love is not an emotion. It is your very existence.

Rather than being your thoughts and emotions, be the awareness behind them.

Your emotions are the slaves to your thoughts, and you are the slave to your emotions.

I keep my emotions buried under the floor. Locked up deep, where they can't hurt me any more.

No emotion is the final one. - Jeanette Winterson

Reason generates the list of possibilities. Emotion chooses from that list. –Dale Peterson

Emotion is energy in motion. - Peter McWilliams

When you welcome your emotions as teachers, every emotion brings good news, even the ones that are painful.

Human behavior flows from three main sources: desire, emotion, and knowledge. –Plato

I haven't got that kind of discipline where I can turn my emotion inside out and then just switch off. It affects me fairly profoundly and I don't like putting myself through that kind of mincer every day. -Jimmy Nail

Negative emotions like hatred destroy our peace of mind. - Matthew Ricard

Wit is the epitaph of an emotion. –Friedrich Nietzsche

Unexpressed emotions will never die. They are buried alive and will come forth later in uglier ways. – Sigmund Freud

An emotion can best be viewed as an energy that comes to you for healing.

And if thought and emotion can persist in this way so long after the brain that sent them forth has crumpled into dust, how vitally important it must be to control their very birth in the heart, and guard them with the keenest possible restraint.-Algernon Blackwood

Emotion is the poetry of life.

Quotes About Anger

For every minute you are angry, you lose sixty seconds of happiness.

Anger makes you smaller, while forgiveness forces you to grow beyond what you were.

The one that angers you controls you. Don't give anyone that power. Especially the one who does it intentionally?

Holding on to anger is like grasping a hot coal with the intent of throwing it at someone else; you are the one who gets burned. -Buddha

You can keep a sword or a gun but never have to use it; so it is with anger.

A person who has lots of anger inside, definitely loves people more than anyone else can. Because if red color indicates anger then it indicates love too.

Sometimes the words we say in anger are the words we really meant to say but kept inside for so long.

Anger is an acid that can do more harm to the vessel in which it is stored than to anything on which it is poured. Mark Twain

Anybody can become angry-that is easy, but to be angry with the right person and to the right degree and at the right time and for the right purpose, and in the right way-that is not within everybody's power and is not easy. –Aristotle

Anger dwells only in the bosom of fools. - Albert Einstein

Anger is a killing thing. It kills the man who angers, for each rage leaves him less than he had been before. It takes something from him. - Louis L Armour

In a controversy the instant we feel anger we have already ceased striving for the truth, and have begun striving for ourselves. Buddha

Bitterness is like cancer. It eats upon the host. But anger is like fire. It burns it all clean. –Maya Angelou

For every minute you remain angry, you give up sixty seconds of peace of mind. –Ralph Waldo Emerson

Speak when you are angry and you will make the best speech you will ever regret. –Ambrose Bierce

In times of great stress or adversity, it's always best to keep busy, to plow your anger and your energy into something positive. -Lee Iacocca

Getting angry is actually punishing yourself with the mistakes of others.

Whatever is begun in anger ends in shame.-Benjamin Franklin

When anger rises, think of the consequences.-Confucius

People won't have time for you if you are always angry or complaining.-Stephen Hawking

When you are offended at any man's fault, turn to yourself and study your own failings. Then you will forget your anger. -Epictetus

Get mad then get over it. –Colin Powell

Anger is only one letter short of Danger.

Don't get the impression that you arouse my anger. You see, one can only be angry with those he respects. –Richard M Nixon

Usually when people are sad, they don't do anything they just cry over their condition. But when they get angry, they bring about change.

The more anger toward the past you carry in your heart, the less capable you are of loving in the present.

Anger doesn't solve anything. It builds nothing, but it can destroy everything.

Be not angry that you cannot make others as you wish them to be, since you cannot make yourself as you wish to be. –Thomas A. Kempis

We can't let the anger overshadow the good things in life.

Life is short, live it. Love is rare, grab it. Anger is bad, dump it. Fear is awful, face it. Memories are sweet, cherish them.

Make your anger so expensive that no one can ever afford it, and make your happiness so cheap that everyone can get it for free from you.

Sometimes you say things out of emotion and anger to the ones you love the most. When it drives them away, all you can do is change and hope for them to remember the good in you that always outweighs the bad.

Never reply when you are angry. Never make a promise when you are happy. Never make a decision when you are sad.

Don't live your life with anger and hate in your heart. You'll only be hurting yourself more than the people you hate.

For every minute you remain angry, you give up sixty seconds of peace of mind. –Ralph Waldo Emerson

Anger is our natural defense against pain. So when I say I hate you, it really means you hurt me.

Anger is your biggest enemy. Control it.

It's better to cry than to be angry; because anger hurts others, while tears flow silently through the soul and cleanses the heart. Pope John Paul II

Let your love be stronger than your hate or anger.

Learn the wisdom of compromise, for it is better to bend a little than to break.

H.A.T.E.R.S: Having Anger Toward Everyone Reaching Success

Overcoming Depression Quotes

To My Illness: I'm not fretting over you an hour, a minute, or even a second longer. I'm too busy getting stronger.

Don't let your struggle become your identity.

Depression is merely anger without enthusiasm.

I am stronger than depression.

When something bad happens, you have three choices. You can either let it define you, let it destroy you, or you can let it strengthen you.

Wake up every morning with the thought that something wonderful is about to happen.

Depression taught me the importance of compassion and hard work, and that you can overcome enormous obstacles. -Rob Delaney

The bravest thing I ever did was continuing my life when I wanted to die.

Although the world is full of struggle, it is also full of overcoming it.

Don't believe everything you think.

The only good luck many great men ever had was being born with the ability and determination to overcome bad luck. –Channing Pollock

Before you can see the light, you have to deal with the darkness.

Don't worry about what people say behind your back, they are the people who are finding faults in your life instead of fixing the faults in their own life.

Just when the caterpillar thought the world was over, it became a butterfly.

Talking about our problems is our greatest addiction. Break the habit. Talk about your joys.

Your success is measured by the strength of your desire, the size of your dream, and how you handle disappointment along the way.

Be still, sad heart! And cease repining; behind the clouds is the sun still shining; thy fate is the common fate of all, into each life some rain must fall.

When you have positive thoughts, embrace them. When you have negative thoughts, push them out of your mind by focusing.

Our greatest weakness lies in giving up. The most certain way to succeed is always to try just one more time. –Thomas Edison

If you run into a wall, don't turn around and give up. Figure out how to climb it, go through it, or work around it. –Michael Jordan

Quotes about Stress

Dear stress, let's break up.

In times of great stress or adversity, it's always best to keep busy, to plow your anger and your energy into something positive. -Lee Iacocca

Don't think too much. You'll create a problem that wasn't even there in the first place.

Much of the stress that people feel doesn't come from having too much to do. It comes from not finishing what they've started.-David Allen

Embrace the current season in your life. It's only temporary.

Stress is basically a disconnection from the earth, a forgetting of the breath. Stress is an ignorant state. It believes that everything is an emergency. Nothing is that important. Just lie down. -Natalie Goldberg

It's not the load that breaks you down, it's the way you carry it.

Stop worrying about what you have to lose and start focusing on what you have to gain.

When you're stressed, you eat ice cream, chocolate, and sweets. You know why? Because stressed spelled backward is desserts.

It's not the stress that kills us, it's our reaction to it. - Hans Selye

The major cause of stress is the inability of people to discover their real nature. Discover your gifts, follow them and you will never feel stressed.

Give your stress wings and let it fly away. –Terri Guillemets

Brain cells create ideas. Stress kills brain cells. Stress is not a good idea.- Frederick Sounders

Do not worry about the past or the future. This moment needs your attention, for this is where your life exists.

The greatest weapon against stress is our ability to choose one thought over another.- William James

Why is there so much stress in life? It's because we focus too much on improving our lifestyle rather than our life.

Saying yes to happiness means learning to say no to things and people that stress you out. –Thema Davis

Don't stress. Look up to God. Hand it back to him and He will turn it all around.

Book 3

Lord Deliver Me from Negative Health Talk: A Guide to Speaking Healing Words of Faith

Lynn R Davis

PUBLISHED BY

Lynn R Davis
Copyright © 2013
Be the first to know when my books are free. Register your email at:
http://www.LynnRDavis.com

All rights reserved.

No part of this publication may be copied, reproduced in any format, by any means, electronic or otherwise, without prior consent from the copyright owner and publisher of this book.

Table of Contents

Dedication

Introduction

1-Unhealthy Words We Say About Ourselves

2-Unhealthy Words We Say About Others

3-Unhealthy Words Others Say About You

4- Are You Willing To Participate?

5- WDJD – What did Jesus Do? The Jesus Factor

6-Final Words of Encouragement

7-Daily Inspiration and Scripture Meditations

Author and Book Information

Dedication

I still believe breast cancer was defeated on the cross.

This is the type of book that I wish I could have given to my Auntie, my best friend, during her three year faith fight against breast cancer.

Would it have made a difference? Only she and God know the answer. Most of the examples in this book will be based on her experiences and our communications together that lead me to share her story.

Though the wound is fresh and I occasionally shed tears as I write, I am not without hope. The joy of the Lord is my strength. And I will let nothing separate me from His love.

Make no mistake; I still believe that breast cancer was defeated on the cross. And I know my Auntie would agree.

My heart tells me this book will make a difference for someone. I don't know for whom. I pray that it is you.

God bless.

I Love You Auntie
Mrs. Johnnie Mae Bradshaw
November 8, 1962 to October 8, 2012

Introduction

If you can't say something healing, don't say anything at all.

This is a book about healing words. Much like the first book, "Deliver Me From Negative Self-talk," it is based on scripture and biblical principles for governing our conversation in such a way that we speak life and not death - over ourselves and others.

The main focus of this book though, is health and healing. Often a controversial subject because some believers don't think healing is for the modern church, while others believe it is but just think God practices "selective healing" at His discretion.

Still, some Christians believe in healing and desperately want it, but they talk themselves out it. Their health talk is so negative that they sabotage the manifestation of their own healing.

Based on what I've read and studied, I believe healing is for everyone. So why do some receive healing while others do not? I don't have that answer. And I question whether or not I should know.

Maybe I haven't reached that level of wisdom in my spiritual journey - yet. I don't know, but I continue to pray for wisdom on this subject and others.

Don't Talk Yourself Out Of Health

I would tell my aunt every day, "Don't talk yourself out of your healing." But helping her stay motivated got really difficult when her hair fell out from the chemo. "I'm bald-headed," she'd say, "I know I look bad."

I tried to reassure her, "You're beautiful and besides,

you love wigs anyway."

I reminded her that her hair would grow back thicker and more beautiful than ever (and it did).

My aunt was super talented in many areas; gardening, carpentry, floral design, and hair styling. And being the creative kitchen stylist she was, she fashioned a wig made of human hair that fit her perfectly. She regained her confidence and her faith was renewed. She took her focus off of losing her hair and began concentrating on her health - at least for a little while.

A beautiful woman inside and out, Auntie took great pride in her appearance. But as some of you know, cancer doesn't care about your inner or outer beauty. Cancer is a relentless bully.

Auntie handled the mastectomy. She hid the scars beneath fashionable clothing. She wore gorgeous wigs that complimented her beautifully. But it was when a tumor grew above her eye causing it to nearly close shut, that I saw her faith wane the most.

When her grandchildren pointed and asked, "Grandma what's wrong with your eye?" she became frustrated and didn't answer. She knew they were just toddlers and they didn't understand what was happening to their grandma. But I believe the constant reminder of her condition was too overwhelming.

The enemy likes to keep our problems in front of us at all times. He wants to rub our condition in our faces so that we lose faith and hope in healing.

When you have a condition that draws attention from others, it can be difficult to overcome the questions and pointing fingers. But we must remember that the enemy is using whatever he can to destroy our faith. Our focus must be on what we cannot see.

I remember hearing how Dodie Osteen, diagnosed with metastatic cancer of the liver at age 48, posted pictures of herself all around from her horseback riding days, the days when she was strong, healthy, and happy. She placed her focus on those images and refused to see herself as sick or deteriorating. She had a vision because she understood, "without a vision the people perish." Dodie is now in her late 70's. God is good!

The greater the health challenge the more difficult it can be to remain faithful and positive. We become so tempted to say what we see, which is the exact opposite of what faith is. Faith believes in something we cannot see with the natural eye.

Faith is looking at your fragile, deteriorating body in the mirror and saying, "By His stripes I am healed," "I am made in His image and I am fearfully and wonderfully made."

And though the physical body may not look wonderful, your spirit is wonderful and whole. And it is your faith that will restore your body to its wholeness.

The enemy knows each of us well. He knows what our weak points are. Just like he knew that Auntie was a proud woman who took pride in her appearance. The enemy will attack you in the area that he knows is likely to challenge your faith the most.

But you must stay vigilant. Recognize what is happening. "Lest Satan should get an advantage of us: for we are not ignorant of his devices." 2 Cor. 2:11

I want to introduce this book with a few words of exhortation and encouragement. You Have Power. You Have Favor. You Have Jesus. Don't Give Up!

"I set before you life and death. Choose life."
(Deuteronomy 30:19)

You have the power of choice. Make the decision to be healed. You have to choose life. It's not just a default response. Our human nature tends to lean toward the negative. Choose life.

"Life and death are in the power of the tongue."
(Proverbs 18:21)

You have power to call those things that be not as though they were. Use it to claim your healing and proclaim that Jesus is Lord of your life. Use your power to praise God for the healing He has promised you.

Use the power of your tongue to rejoice in the face of adversity to show the enemy that you will not give up on God, because God is mindful of you and He has not given up on you. Amen!

"Be ye transformed by the renewing of your mind..."

An old dog can learn new tricks. Your mind is not set in stone. Your mind can be transformed and renewed. And your renewed mind will take you into a place of healing and provision. A place that your old carnal, negative-thinking mind cannot even imagine.

The word is life to those who find it and health to their flesh. Believe in the word, not the world. "I have told you these things, so that in me you may have peace. In this world you will have trouble. But take heart! I have overcome the world." (John 16:33)

"The word is a lamp unto my feet and a light to my path." (Psalm 119:105)

Know that there is a path to follow. The bible says there is a way that seems right to men, but the end is destruction. It may seem right to expect death from sickness and disease, but that is not the will of God. Know that God has another plan for your life. That plan is an abundant life. Jesus came that we might have life more abundantly. There is a path to follow and He will guide you if you let Him.

"For the vision is yet for an appointed time; But at the end it will speak, and it will not lie. Though it tarries, wait for it; because it will surely come, it will not tarry." (Habakkuk 2:3)

Don't you dare give up! God is not caught off guard by your illness. He knew it was going to happen before you were born. He knew it was going to happen the day His son was nailed to the cross. You are the reason His son suffered and died. There is an appointed time for your healing. Though it may not look like it. Though it may not happen immediately, "it will surely come!"

I hope that you are encouraged and ready to get started.

1-Unhealthy Words We Say About Ourselves

Everything is made of something that we cannot see. Did you know that our words have energy? Sound is vibration. And vibration is energy. In the beginning, God spoke his energy and the universe came into existence.

Your attitude, words, and actions are energy which when released into your atmosphere, cause things to happen. You have to admit that words can change the mood of any setting.

A yelling parent can set children on edge and make them nervous and even ill. And words don't just affect people. Studies have shown that words effect plant growth. They actually thrive when you talk to them. Words change environments!

You can't speak sickness and death and expect healing. It's important to nurture your environment with positivity and the best way to do that is through the energy of your words. Avoid rehearsing the worst case scenario or what the doctor said could happen. Reject the negative thoughts that try to creep in whenever you feel pain or see a lump, lesion, or sore.

Speak life-giving words, "By His stripes I am healed," "My god is my refuge and a very present help."

Help My Unbelief

Human faith relies on five senses, but supernatural faith relies on the power of the word. "The word is life to those who find it and health to their flesh."

Walk by faith not sight. Setbacks happen. Don't be distracted by negative reports. Remember God's promise; "I know the plans I have for you. Plans to give you a future…" (Jeremiah 29:11)

Positive Health Talk Examples

Don't Say: I'm going to die.
Do Say: I shall live and declare the works of the Lord. (Psalm 118:17)

Don't Say: My health is getting worse.
Do Say: I am a believer and not a doubter. I believe I am healed no matter what I am experiencing. (Hebrews 11:1)

Don't Say: There's an epidemic, I'm probably going to catch it.
Do Say: I have the authority to overcome the power of the enemy. No epidemic shall harm me. (Luke 10:19)

Don't Say: My high blood pressure; my diabetes; my cancer.
Do Say: The Lord is removing from me all sickness and disease.(Deut. 7: 12)

Don't Say: This job is going to give me a heart attack!
Do Say: I work for the glory of God, not man. My work will be rewarded. (Col 3:23) (2 Chronicles 5:17)

Don't Say: These children are going to be the death of me.
Do Say: The grace of God is in me. My children arise and call me blessed. (Romans 16:20) (Proverbs 31:28)

Don't Say: I will never be whole again.
Do Say: My mind, body, and soul are restored and I am made whole by the power of Jesus through faith.

Don't Say: The treatments aren't working and there is nothing else the doctors can do.
Do Say: By His stripes I am healed. It is the Lord that heals me. (Ex.15:26) (Is. 53:5)

Don't Say: God hasn't healed me yet. Maybe healing is not for me.
Do Say: The Lord is full of compassion and mercy. And I patiently expect a total healing. (James 5:10-11)

2-Unhealthy Words We Say About Others

Maybe you're in a situation like I was. Someone you love dearly is ill and you feel helpless to do anything. You may not be able to take away their pain or make their disease go away, but you can pray and stand in faith with them.

I watched an interesting documentary once that showed people who had others praying for them healed faster than those who were going through their illness alone. "The prayers of the righteous avails much."(James 5:16)

Sickness and disease often progress over a period of time. And often the healing process is progressive as well. Don't be discouraged if you lay hands on someone and there is no immediate physical indication of healing.

This reminds me of Jesus cursing the tree and commanding the roots to dry up. At that moment nothing visibly changed about the tree at first. That's because the change started beneath the ground in the roots - invisible to the eye. The next day the tree was dead.

That is what I believe about some sickness and disease. Prayer begins to work when we believe. We may not see it, but we must believe it in order to receive. "Believe when you receive it, when you pray, you shall have whatsoever you ask." (Matthew 21:22)

Be Supportive

When someone you know is going through a health challenge, be supportive. When they are down, lift them up. Don't share negative experiences, share positive ones. Don't bombard them with your internet research on death statistics, share healing testimonies and research successful new innovations.

Do whatever you can to help them enter into a place of rest, to be at peace. My aunt used to tell me that she loved for me to visit because she always felt better after I left. People should feel better when you leave them. They shouldn't feel drained.

I'm not trying to make you feel bad. I just want you to be aware that your words matter. The things that you are saying could be hurting your loved one's chances of experiencing the healing they've been praying for.

God's favor and grace should shine through in your words, actions, and attitude. They shouldn't see you distraught, in tears, and hopeless. And by all means, they should never feel as though you have given up on them. I knew a lady who was visited in the hospital by a few church members. She said during the visit they started asking her questions about the type of program she wanted at her funeral!

Our words should always agree with the word of God. Regardless of how bad things look or difficult the situation, we should always be loving, supportive, and faithful. During the critical moments of a person's life we must be sure that we are speaking life, not death (Proverbs 10:20).

"Most of us, swimming against the tides of trouble the world knows nothing about, need only a bit of praise or encouragement - and we will make the goal." - Jerome Fleishman

Positive Health Talk Examples

Don't Say: Yeah, right! There's no cure for what you have.
Do Say: I agree with you in Jesus name, by His stripes you are healed and made whole.(Matthew 18:19)

Don't Say: You're only going to get worse.
Do Say: The Lord is restoring health unto you. He is healing your (insert heart, mind, body, etc). (Jeremiah 30:17)

Don't Say: The doctor said you're never going to (walk, talk, see, etc.) again.
Do Say: You can do all things through Christ who strengthens your (legs, arms, eyes, mind, etc).(Philippians 4:13)

Don't Say: God must be punishing you for something.
Do Say: God loves you. You are forgiven. And By His stripes you are healed. (Psalm 105:3)

Don't Say: They have one foot in the grave.
Do Say: The same Spirit that raised Christ from the dead lives in you and is strengthening your physical body.(Romans 8:11)

3-Unhealthy Words Others Say About You

Sarah and her husband Marcus, an assistant minister, spent time with my aunt in the hospital just before she was to be transported to a hospice house for "therapy." During the visit, Auntie said she was feeling sad and defeated. She didn't want go to hospice. She felt that's where people go to die. Though death was heavy on her mind, during Sarah and Marcus' visit she tried to be her usual upbeat self.

After Sarah and Marcus left, Auntie said she felt drained. She turned off the overhead light to help her rest, but just as the room darkened the door opened. It was Marcus.

She clicked the lamp switch, "Hey, did you forget something?" she looked over in the area where Marcus and Sarah had been sitting.

"No. I was driving home, but God told me to come back." Auntie said he looked nervous and kept shifting his eyes downward.

"Why?" She was anxious to hear what he had to say. She expected to hear a statement, but instead Marcus asked her question.

"What is it that you want God to do?"

She recalled the question caught her off guard but said she responded immediately, "I want Him to heal me."

Without saying a word, she said Marcus opened his bible and began to read. The story was about a man named Hezekiah who was told by a prophet that he was going to die. But Hezekiah turned to the wall and prayed to God. At the end of the scripture, the Lord heard Hezekiah and granted him 15 more years to live.

When he'd finished reading (Isaiah 38:2-5), she said Marcus closed his bible and said, "Ms. Johnnie, God told me to tell you, Just Believe".

Auntie said she was sure Marcus must have thought she was crazy because she immediately burst into tears. When she finally reassured him she was okay and that she was just overwhelmed by the word, Marcus left.

That was a great day for her. She cherished those words. She had me read Isaiah 38 to her again as I sat near her bedside.

God Be True and Every Man A Liar (Romans 3:4)

I told her that was a word from God specifically for her. And that she should hold on to that word and believe it with all of her heart. I told her that the enemy would try to convince her to doubt. I told her that her victory was in the word. We prayed and I thanked God for sending her a word that she could hold on to.

Whatever you're facing, there is a word in scripture to address it. A search in your bible concordance or online will yield results containing verses that pertain to subjects like healing, peace, deliverance, and more. In some cases the Holy Spirit may prompt someone close to you to give you a word of encouragement. Or you may hear just what you need on television or in a song.

Whether you receive a word through study, meditation, or inspiration of the Holy Spirit, you hold on to that word. And no matter what anyone else says or does, remember God cannot lie. His word is always true.

Don't Let the Enemy Steal Your Seed (Promise)

Just getting the word is not enough. You have to really believe it. Stand on it. Protect it and allow it to grow and produce healing in your body. The enemy will do anything and use anyone in his power to get you to try and uproot the word that you are standing on. Don't "be ignorant of his devices."

"The sower soweth the word. And these are they by the way side, where the word is sown; but when they have heard, Satan cometh immediately, and taketh away the word that was sown in their hearts." (Mark 4: 14-15)

Mark 4 warns us that the enemy is waiting to steal the word as soon as it is sown in our hearts. He doesn't want the word to produce victory. He comes to steal, kill and destroy.

As soon as you are given a word of promise, the enemy will send some negative naysayer to steal your joy, kill your faith, and destroy your chance of victory.

The day after Marcus told my aunt that God said Just believe, a hospice nurse that Auntie never met told her that she only had six months to live and that she should prepare for such. The enemy had come to steal the word.

Doctors will report what they know. People are going to say what they see. It's one of the challenges we face with human logic.

Friends and family may mean well but sometimes...

They say things that do more harm than good. First I want to say, anyone who loves you will never intentionally say words that will harm you. The people closest to us have the greatest ability to do the most harm. We love them, trust them and listen to them. The enemy knows that and will use it to his advantage. Remember it was Job's wife who told him to curse God and die.

I mentioned in the first book Deliver Me from Negative Self-Talk, about a friend who told me I could "stroke out and die" because I was diagnosed with high blood pressure. Others told me I'd be on medication for the rest of my life and could develop heart disease. They even told me stories about people who died at a young age.

It was horrible, the things they were saying. Somehow they thought they were being helpful by informing me of these pessimistic things. If they weren't feeding me negative stories; they pitied me with "you poor thing," "take it easy, you don't want to overdo it."

Whether the negativity is coming from a lifelong friend, spouse, aunt, uncle child, or favorite cousin - God is not directing this communication. They are speaking from a place of fear and "God has not given us a spirit of fear." It's important that you understand and discern this.

I know you love them, but if they are not encouraging you to hold fast to your healing, you're going to have to politely (in love) correct them (aka put them in their place). Your health depends on it.

Protect Your Mind

When you are standing in faith for your healing, you can't afford to let your mind run wild with thoughts of suffering, death, and dying. There is going to be so much information thrown at you from professionals, family, friends, the internet, media, etc. And the majority of the information will be negative.

When my aunt was first diagnosed with breast cancer, she'd tell me how almost every day someone was either calling or showing up to tell her about someone they knew who died of cancer or had both breasts removed or who suffered some terrible side-effect from the medication or therapy.

She heard so much negativity that she had dreams at night and she said in her sleep she would replay the conversations over and over again and wake up sweating.

I suggested to her what I'm going to suggest to you, stop negative people in their tracks. When people come to you with stories of death and suffering, stop them mid-sentence and say, "I'm in faith for my healing and I only want to hear survival stories and positive testimonies. Do you know any? I'd love to hear some."

My aunt didn't feel comfortable stopping people. She let people talk because she didn't want to be rude (sigh). She was concerned about hurting them, but they were killing her faith with their negativity. Their words were polluting her mind. No one has a right to pollute your mind.

You have to make a decision to block this negative noise pollution. Or it will damage your thinking about your healing and make you begin to wonder, "Will I die like they did?" or "Am I going to get worse? Maybe I should be planning my funeral?"

Like my aunt, you will replay these thoughts conversations over and over in your mind until worry and stress begin to worsen your body's condition. Negative thoughts feed illness in your body and create clouds of doubt - doubt murders faith.

Recognize these attacks on your mind for what they are

- a ploy of the enemy to steal, kill, and destroy your faith.

"Lest Satan should get an advantage of us: for we are not ignorant of his devices." 2: Corinthians 2:11

It's not about hurting anyone's feelings. It's about knowing the enemy. He hits below the belt. He stabs from behind. And he kicks you when you're down. He will use people closest to you to hurt you. Remember when Jesus told Peter, "Get behind me Satan?" It wasn't because He thought Peter was a devil. It was because He recognized that the enemy was influencing Peter's words.

Those who truly love you will understand your faith. Their feelings won't be hurt because you express your desire for healing. They probably don't know that the enemy is using their negativity to hinder your faith.

Those whose feelings are hurt, well…you are better off not communicating with them anyway. It sounds harsh. But love them, pray for them, and love them from a distance. For healing to take place, outside of a miracle, you need an environment of peace, love, and a sound mind. None of which will come from listening to negative naysayers all day.

Take the phone off the hook. Lock your doors. Change your number if you have to. But by all means, while you believe for your healing, protect your ears and your mind from negativity. I repeat, some people you will just have to love from a distance.

Your medical professionals have God-given skills and talent but…

They don't have the last word. I respect the medical profession a great deal. Doctors are a blessing to society and without them many more lives would be lost than we can imagine. I believe that God has worked through millions of physicians and nurses to facilitate marvelous healing and recovery.

Luke, writer of the third and longest gospel, was a physician by profession. Don't you find it intriguing that a book of the New Testament was written by a doctor? I think that's awesome! Jesus had a doctor in His midst and there is nothing wrong with you having positive, committed, and experienced healing professionals in your midst either. But I digress…

Like I was saying, physicians have a job to do - to report the facts as they understand them based on years of intense study and research. They give the worst case scenario and do what is within their means to prevent illness and preserve life. Thank God for them!

My doctors are great. I respect them. And I prayerfully follow their instructions. When I've been prescribed medications, I've taken them. But I have never accepted that I will have to take any medication forever.

I suppose my perspective is a bit different than most. I believe doctors are giving me the information I need to direct my prayers and focus my faith. How else would I know to pray specifically about blood platelet counts, lymph nodes, or blocked arteries?

Sometimes our prayers need to be focused. And the information doctors share can help us hone in the cause of our illnesses much better than we could otherwise. I believe once they give us information, we shouldn't just leave and say, "That's it. I'm going to die."

I believe we should listen. Ask questions. Get as much information as possible. And leave knowing that the name of Jesus is above every name. While a negative report may be the doctor's final word, it's not God's.

God has the last word

I was very angry when my aunt told me that her home health nurse told her she would never walk again and that the swelling in her abdomen would never go away. My aunt was terribly upset.

Though she had no sensation from her hips down, she believed she would walk again. She believed so strongly that she allowed her son to help her with therapeutic exercises. She made plans for planting new rose bushes and reestablishing her garden. But after the nurse told her emphatically that those things would never happen, Auntie began to shut down again.

She didn't say she was giving up, but I could hear it in her tone when she would say things like, "Why do the exercises if I'm never going to walk again."

Auntie stopped trying. She stopped hoping. She stopped believing.

I was blessed by Dodie Osteen's testimony of her healing from liver cancer. She was basically told that she had six months to live and was sent home to live out her last days with family. Dodie did not take that as the final word. She instead went into prayer with her family and made up her mind that Jesus' name was above the name of cancer.

She meditated on healing scriptures daily. And from what I understand, she still does. I believe she decided to "let God be truth and every man a liar." She decided that God's word was the last word. Progressively she began to improve and eventually, over a period of time, was diagnosed to be cancer free.

She prayed. She hoped. She believed. God was true and every man was a liar. Man will give you an expiration date, but God will give you inspiration! Be healed Jesus' name.

Positive Health Talk Examples

They Shouldn't Say: What exactly did the doctor say is wrong with you?
They Should Say: No weapon formed against you shall prosper. I'm standing in agreement with you for your healing. (Isaiah 54:17)

They Shouldn't Say: You've been sick a long time. You're really bad off."
They Should Say: God is restoring you and making you strong.(1Peter 5:10)

They Shouldn't Say: You should just accept it (illness).
They Should Say: I believe you are loosed from (illness) in Jesus' name.(Luke 13:12)

(Be sure to revisit previous chapter examples as well as the more extensive list of examples in Book 1, *Deliver Me From Negative Self Talk*.)

4- Are You Willing To Participate?

Faith and action work together

"Faith without works is dead," has been used in many contexts. I believe it applies anytime we are standing in faith for a breakthrough. And a desire for healing certainly qualifies.

Years ago when my blood pressure sky-rocketed because of stress and poor diet, I was diagnosed with high blood pressure (HBP) and prescribed meds. I began to pray and ask God what to do. But in the meantime, I took the medication. I didn't refer to HBP as "my high blood pressure." God didn't give it to me. I didn't want it. And I wasn't claiming it.

I went home and did my research. Learned about exercise, foods, and vitamins that were beneficial for HBP and once I cleared the supplements with my doctor, I got busy. I had faith that I would be free of HBP. I did my part (faith without works is dead). And after a time, was eventually taken off HBP medication.

"You see that his faith and his actions were working together, and his faith was made complete by what he did." James 2:22

In James 2:22, Paul talks about Abraham's phenomenal display of faith when he offered his beloved son Isaac as a sacrifice.

I believe this applies to us in our health. Sometimes our breakthrough requires sacrifice on our part. Whether the act of sacrifice is walking 30 minutes per day, abstaining from chocolate covered donuts, or going to bed an hour early for more rest.

If we believe for healing, we must be willing to put action with our faith. "Faith without works is like a bird without wings; though she may hop with her companions on earth, yet she will never fly with them to heaven." - Francis Beaumont

God Respects Your Free Will

If we want to eat fat, grease, and salt; we can. That's our right. God respects your free will. Just like he doesn't force us to receive salvation, He won't force us to eat right, get enough rest, or exercise. There comes a point in time when a person has to make a choice. They have to want change, want to receive help, and want to believe.

God is not going to show up at your dining room table and remove the fork from your hand to keep you from stuffing yourself. Nor will He seal your mouth shut when you lean back, pat your stomach and grunt, "All this fried chicken is going to give me a heart attack."

He won't stop you from saying, "My kids are sending me to an early grave!" Nor will he force you to schedule your annual physical exams, rest properly, etc. You get the point.

He respects our right to worry, stress, argue, and over-react to every negative situation that comes our way. He doesn't like it. He doesn't agree with it. But He has given you free will to make your own choices.

"I've set before you life and death, blessing and cursing. Choose life so that you and your seed may live." Deuteronomy 30:19

God will not force us to seek peace. But we have to understand that there are consequences in choosing otherwise. Stress opens the door for natural illnesses and health complications; physical, emotional, and psychological.

5- WDJD – What did Jesus Do? The Jesus Factor

When we think of Jesus we tend to mainly think of Him at his death, burial, and resurrection in the since that he delivered us from eternal damnation (John 3:17).

We believe that we have eternal life in heaven because of Jesus, but we don't fully believe that we have a right to a healthy, healed, and blessed life on earth.

"The son of God was manifested that he might destroy the works of the devil." (1 John3:8)

Sickness and disease, whether physical or mental, is the work of the enemy - your enemy. Jesus, the word, was made flesh and was born as a man to destroy your sickness and disease.

Lay aside every weight. Stay focused. Know that giants do fall. Jesus is the creator of life, grace, redemption. (John 20:31 and Philippians 4:6-7)

Live like you have an inheritance. The bible is the will and Jesus left you an inheritance of healing, wealth, peace, and salvation. It's in the Will (of God). You're entitled to health and healing.

"He himself bore our sins in his body on the tree, so that we might die to sins and live for righteousness; by his wounds you have been healed." (1Peter 2:24)

He Has Pardoned You

Auntie called me one day and I could tell she was upset. Someone, she wouldn't say who, had visited that afternoon to "check on her." During the conversation the person suggested that sickness and disease is a form of punishment from God.

"They actually said that to you?" My voice rose a bit and my temples thumped.

She sensed my agitation, "No, Lynn-Lynn, calm down. They didn't say it directly. They just kind of hinted at it."

"Who was it?" I was half ready to give them a piece of my mind.

I think she knew that. She wouldn't tell me. Not wanting to make matters worse, I didn't press. "Auntie some people are ignorant. Jesus died for our healing. Why would God contradict His own son by punishing us with sickness?"

She was still doubtful, but she sounded better. "So you don't think I got breast cancer because God was punishing me?"

"No Auntie. I don't believe that. And you shouldn't either. God loves you. Nothing you've done wrong is bigger than what Jesus did on the cross." I was glad she couldn't see me. Tears rolled down my cheeks. I felt powerless. I wished I could somehow protect her from every negative, ignorant person on the planet.

By the end of our conversation, she seemed better, but I knew that damage had been done. A seed of doubt had been planted. That person's words were lingering in her mind and she was now questioning whether the God she wanted to heal her was actually punishing her for something she'd done wrong.

We must be cautious with assigning blame and making assumptions about what is happening in other people's lives (and our own).

We should never assume that because God doesn't stop something, that He is causing it or condoning it. Neither is true. I just don't believe that.

I prayed for Auntie's understanding. I prayed God's love would abound in her heart and she would know the truth of Jesus and that she would be set free.

He Forgave You

"Bless the Lord, O my soul, who forgiveth all thine iniquities, who healteth all thy diseases." (Psalm 103:3)

Don't let your past mistakes convince you that you deserve to be sick. Jesus forgives and heals (Psalms 103:3). Once you ask for forgiveness and forgive others, you can, by faith, take hold of your healing with confidence. Find healing verses in scripture and meditate on them. And say like Jacob, "I won't let go until you bless me!" (Genesis 32:26)

He Saved You

Yes, Jesus died for your salvation. You can't see it. But you believe you are saved. Have the same faith in your healing. Though you have prayed for it; you may not see it right away, but I urge you to believe you are healed.

That's one of the things my aunt and I talked about quite often. I asked her one day, "What would you say if your oncologist told you that you were not saved?"

Without missing a beat she blurted, "He can't tell me I'm not saved." She was sure of her salvation. She was positive that Jesus had saved her and she was going to heaven.

I wanted her to see her healing in the same manner, "Exactly," I leaned forward, "and no doctor can tell you that Jesus hasn't already healed you either."

Jesus took your sickness upon His body on the cross. He suffered for your healing. Receive it by faith. He's ready to forgive you of your sins and heal you of your diseases (Psalms 103:3).

Salvation is just part of your blessing. If someone gave you a gift, would you cut it in half and give part of it back? Of course not, but we so often only accept half of our inheritance. We receive salvation by faith, but the remainder of our blessing; we choose to leave behind.

Prayer: "Father forgive me for doubting your word. I repent of my sins. I forgive those who have wronged me and I believe I am forgiven. Thank you for your mercy, grace, and comforting Spirit. I receive my healing right now through the mighty name of Jesus. By His stripes I was healed and I am now made whole, in Jesus name, Amen."

Be Steadfast Unmovable

Cast your cares on Him and turn your focus toward healing. He cares for you (1 Peter 5:7). Turn your focus toward healing. Be steadfast and unmovable in your faith. When you trust in someone, you feel secure, calm, and reassured.

That's how we should feel about the word of God - secure, calm, and reassured.

"Blessed assurance, Jesus is mine! Oh, what a foretaste of glory divine! Heir of salvation, purchase of God, Born of His Spirit, washed in His blood." - Hymn lyrics (1873) by Fanny J. Crosby

Be assured that His healing power is as much for you today as it was for the woman with the issue of blood (Matthew 9), the lame man at the gate called Beautiful (Acts 3), the man with the withered hand (Mark 3), or Peter's mother-in-law sick with fever (Matthew 8).

Be hopeful and positive. Hope is seeing something that isn't there. It's seeing yourself healthy and whole. Give thanks to God; not for the illness, but for the grace to overcome and the God's goodness to perform a great work in your life.

Don't look in the mirror on your wall. Look in the mirror of God's grace. See yourself healthy and doing the things you love. And spending time with the people you love. Romans 5:20 says, "Where sin abounds, grace much more abounds." And I believe that where sickness abounds, grace will much more abound!

You're Not Faking It, You're FAITHING It!

Shortly after releasing Deliver Me from Negative Self-Talk, I received several comments. Most of them were, and continue to be, very positive. But one comment in particular described the work as "a little fake it till you make it book."

I admit that I was disappointed by the comment and the rating, but in my heart I knew the truth. Not everyone has received the revelation of Proverbs 18:21. They think you're ignoring reality. My question is whose reality?

The world's reality that says you get sick and you die. Or the reality of the word that says, "By His stripes we are healed."

By choosing healing, you're not denying the illness exists in your body. But you are denying its right to thrive and destroy your life. It is the enemy that steals, kills, and destroys. Illness is from the enemy. Deny it in your words, your thoughts, and your actions.

Don't speak unhealthy words. Don't focus on unhealthy thoughts and images. Let your words, thoughts and actions be those of life and live more abundantly! (John 10:10)

We have a choice to make. It's up to us to decide what our truth is.

Resist opinions that you are delusional or that you are just trying to "fake it until you make it" instead make the chose to "FAITH it until you make it".

There's nothing fake about the word of God. And when you know that your spirit is perfectly healed and whole and the power of God dwells in you; it gives you confidence. There's nothing fake about confidence in God.

There is nothing fake about the word. And there is nothing fake about the death, burial, and resurrection of Jesus Christ. Jesus wasn't faking it and neither are you.

Who Do You Say He Is?

"Who do you say I am?" (16) Simon (Peter) answered, "You are the Messiah, the Son of the living God." (17) Jesus replied, "Blessed are you Simon son of Jonah, for this was not revealed to you by flesh and blood, but by my Father in heaven."

Peter knew without a shadow of a doubt that Jesus was the Son of the living God. Do you know who Jesus is? Do you know what He did for you?

Your physical or emotional illness will not reveal to

you who Jesus is. You must have a relationship with the Lord. You must abide in Him and His word in you.

When the Holy Spirit reveals to you truly who Jesus is and what He did for you, you will accept your healing by faith without fear or reservation. Because you know it is the will of God that you walk in divine health. Who do you say He is?

- I say He is my:
- Savior
- Deliverer
- Counselor
- Healer
- Messiah
- Jehovah
- Mediator
- Prince of Peace
- Redeemer
- Shepherd
- True Vine
- My Rock

6-Final Words of Encouragement

I actually thought I was done, but it is really on my heart to talk about one last thing - REST. Over and over again the word tells us to rest and be at peace.

If you really want to see God work in your life, you're going to have to "rest" in His promises. Trust Him and be at peace about what He has promised you.

And He said, "My presence shall go with you, and I will give you rest." (Exodus 33:14)

God is always with us. He has promised to never leave or forsake us. One of the definitions of rest is "freedom from labor or activity." We are free from works. Our healing is not promised to us because of what great things we have done or how many hours a day we pray.

"Then he answered and spake unto me, saying, this is the word of the LORD unto Zerubbabel, saying, not by might, nor by power, but by my spirit, saith the LORD of hosts." (Zechariah 4:6)

Healing is not a reward, it's a gift. Jesus did all of the work. It is God's power that is at work within you. Jehovah Rapha, the Lord God is your Healer. Call on His name. Confess His word. Rest assured He will deliver you - because He promised. And He cannot lie.

"Come to Me, all who are weary and heavy-laden, and I will give you rest. Take My yoke upon you, and learn from Me, for I am gentle and humble in heart; and you shall find rest for your souls. For My yoke is easy, and My load is light." (Matthew 11:28-30)

You or someone you love may be carrying the heavy burden of sickness and disease. God is saying to you, "come to my Word, I will give you the rest you long for."

Our Father is loving and He wants to replace your heavy burden with His love, joy, and peace. He doesn't want you spinning your wheels and going nowhere. He wants you to be healthy, productive, and working in the kingdom.

The yoke of serving God is far lighter than the yoke of the world. Because Jesus is always there to share your load and help you carry whatever comes upon you. If you're weary today, turn to Jesus. Rest on the promises of God. Let Him help you. Cast your cares on Him. He cares for you!

God bless.

7-Daily Inspiration and Scripture Meditations

It's so important that you spend time meditating on the word of God. "The word is life to those who find it and health to their flesh." You must believe that. God's word will feed your soul (mind, will, imagination, emotions, and intellect).

By feeding your soul the word of God, you will allow the word to work in you. You will allow the Holy Spirit access to comfort, guide, support, and lead you. Your faith pleases God. Faith comes by hearing and hearing by the word. (Romans 10:17)

Use these daily meditations as a starting point. Search your bible for healing scriptures. Study them. Pray over them. Confess them over your life. Thank God for your healing daily. And stand fast on His promise.

Don't give up on God because He has not given up on you.

"God cannot give us a happiness and peace apart from Himself, because it is not there. There is no such thing." (C. S. Lewis)

Day 1 Meditation - Be In Health

Scripture Reading:

"Beloved, I pray that you may prosper in all things and be in health, just as your soul prospers." (3 John 1:2)

Today's Meditation:

Your soul consists of your mind, will, imagination, emotions, and intellect. All of which God wants to prosper. But, God also wants you to prosper in your health. Don't believe the enemy who tells you that you must die of something. God wants you to live a long and prosperous life.

Make the choice today to live the life God wants to you to have. Let God be true and every man a liar. Don't accept the lies of the enemy. Before you can receive healing, you must first believe that it is God's will for your life. Lift the name of Jesus today and every day.

Feed your mind, will, imagination, emotions, and intellect with the word of God. He wants to abide in you. Lift Him up and give Him glory for healing today. By faith call yourself "healthy and prosperous" whether you feel it or not, because in Christ all things, including sickness and disease, are under your feet!

Today's Confession:
Confess His word, "Lord I thank you that I prosper and am in health, even as my soul prospers!"

Today's Inspirational Quote:
"A lot of people say they want to get out of pain, and I'm sure that's true, but they aren't willing to make healing a high priority. They aren't willing to look inside to see the source of their pain in order to deal with it."- Lindsay Wagner

Day 2 Meditation – Don't Worry

Scripture Reading:

"Be anxious for nothing, but in everything by prayer and supplication, with thanksgiving, let your requests be made known to God; and the peace of God, which surpasses all understanding, will guard your hearts and minds through Christ Jesus." (Philippians 4:6-7)

Don't fret, pray. Let God know your concerns about the challenge you face. He cares for you. Thank Him for His love, power, and glory manifesting in your life right now. Thank Him for the peace that is enveloping you and calming you right now, in the name of Jesus. God has not given you a spirit of fear. By faith receive your spirit of power and a sound mind.

The enemy wants you to stress and worry. He wants you to magnify your problem. But scripture says, "Magnify the Lord" not magnify the problem. Rest in His arms today knowing that when you pray He hears you, He is mindful of you, and He is your fortress and strong tower. The Lord is your light and salvation, you have nothing to fear.

Today's Confession

Confess His words, "Father I thank you that I have the peace of God that surpasses all understanding and my mind is powerful and sound."

Today's Inspirational Quote "Healing takes courage, and we all have courage, even if we have to dig a little to find it." -Tori Amos

Day 3 Meditation - You Are Delivered!

Scripture Reading:

"He sent his word, and healed them, and delivered them from their destructions." Psalm 107:20

Today's Meditation:

Sometimes we make bad decisions that bring negative consequences in our emotional or physical health. But God offers hope for us. We are able to break free by receiving His forgiveness. Not because we've suddenly become perfect, but because of His mercy.

You serve a merciful God who is ready to send His word to heal you! He sent His son Jesus - His only begotten son - to heal all your diseases. Every emotional sickness, every psychological illness, every physical health challenge, must bow down and subject itself to the word of God.

Man's wisdom is finite. He knows only what He has been taught. Medical professionals play a part in the healing process, but God knows all. He has promised to send His word, heal you, and deliver you from your destructions.

Don't be condemned today. Repent, receive His forgiveness. It's free you don't have to earn it. Jesus already paid for it. Now lift your hands and offer God a sacrifice of praise for your deliverance!

Today's Confession:

Confess His word, "Lord I thank you for your mercy that is new every morning. I receive your deliverance from destruction and I believe I am healed."

Today's Inspirational Quote:

"There are so many ways to heal. Arrogance may have a place in technology, but not in healing. I need to get out of my own way if I am to heal."- Anne Wilson Schaef

Day 4 Meditation - God Will Make His Word Come True

Scripture Reading:

"Then said the Lord unto me, Thou hast well seen: for I will hasten my word to perform it." (Jeremiah 1:12)

Today's Meditation:

Looking at your circumstances, you may think there is no way things are going to get better. But don't discount God. He is fully aware of what you are facing and He has heard your cry for help.

Just as He told Jeremiah, He is telling you; His word will be fulfilled in your life. He cannot lie.

The promise of healing is not an empty one. His word must accomplish what it is sent forth to do. Stay in faith. God's promise to Jeremiah and to us is that no sickness, disease, or trouble that comes against us will overtake or destroy us. If we trust Him and believe His promise, He is faithful to keep his word. Trust God to show himself mighty in your time of weakness.

Today's Confession:

Confess His word: "Lord I trust you and I believe that even now you are with me helping through every day. I know that you will see me through."

Today's Inspirational Quote:

"Trying to suppress or eradicate symptoms on the physical level can be extremely important, but there's more to healing than that; dealing with psychological, emotional and spiritual issues involved in treating sickness is equally important." -Marianne Williamson

Day 5 Meditation - Resurrection Power Lives In You

Scripture Reading:

"But if the Spirit of him that raised up Jesus from the dead dwell in you, he that raised up Christ from the dead shall also quicken your mortal bodies by his Spirit that dwells in you." (Romans 8:11)

Today's Meditation:

Today's scripture tells us that the same Spirit that raised Christ from the dead lives inside you and me. We have more power within than we realize. When we accepted Christ as our Lord and Savior, His Spirit came to dwell inside us. That same Spirit raised Christ from the dead and can heal our bodies - if we only believe.

You are delivered from death. You are delivered from disease. You are alive unto God the father. And the same power that raised Christ from the dead is dwelling on the inside of you.

Your body is the temple of God. Sickness and disease have no right to overtake your body. Sickness and disease cannot live where Jesus lives!

Today's Confession:

Confess His word: "Lord I thank you that the same Spirit that raised Christ from the dead dwells in me. I receive resurrection in every cell of my body. I am healed. I am healthy. I am delivered from death, in Jesus name."

Today's Inspirational Quote:

"It is reasonable to expect the doctor to recognize that science may not have all the answers to problems of health and healing." - Norman Cousins

Day 6 Meditation – You Can't Win With Physical Might

Scripture Reading:

"For though we walk in the flesh, we do not war according to the flesh. For the weapons of our warfare are not carnal but mighty in God for pulling down strongholds." (2 Corinthians 10:4)

Today's Meditation:

You are created in the image of your Father. He is spirit and likewise you are a sprit living a human existence. The battle you are facing should be fought using spiritual tools. We fight battles using our faith in the word. Our human bodies are weak in comparison to our spiritual bodies. The same power that raised Christ from the dead lives in our spirit and we are mighty and powerful through Him.

God's mighty weapons of faith, hope, love, and prayer are available to us every day to pull down the strongholds of any illness. The Holy Spirit is ready to lead you, comfort you, and encourage you. But we must open our hearts to Him and we must choose to use the weapons God has given us. It is only when we draw closer to God during our time of weakness that He is able to show himself strong during our toughest time.

Make the decision today to fight your war against illness using your spiritual arsenal. You won't win this battle through your own physical might; it will be by the power of the God's spirit that lives in you. "Not by might, nor by power, but by my spirit, saith the Lord." (Zechariah 4:6)

Today's Confession:

Confess His Word: "Father I thank you for the powerful weapons of warfare. I will daily use faith, hope, love, prayer and the guidance of the Holy Spirit to win every battle that I am faced with."

Today's Inspirational Quote:

"Healing does not mean going back to the way things were before, but rather allowing what is now to move us closer to God." - Ram Dass

Day 7 Meditation – God Has Plans for You

Scripture Reading:

"For I know the plans I have for you," declares the Lord, "plans to prosper you and not to harm you, plans to give you hope and a future." Jeremiah 29:11 (NIV)

Today's Meditation:

This is one of my favorite scriptures. I have it posted on my vision board. I recite it at least three times a day and always offer it to others as a word of encouragement. God has a plan for me and you. His plan is to give us hope and a bright future.

The Lord didn't plan for you to be sick. It is His will that we walk in divine health. He doesn't want us to become so ill that it takes a miracle to cure us. He wants every cell that He created in our bodies to be healthy and strong.

If you are experiencing illness, please don't let the enemy tell you that this is what God planned for you. Jeremiah 29:11 reveals God's plan is to prosper you, not make you sick or bedridden. So do not accept sickness and disease as part of your life's plan. Reject it!

Sickness in your body is like an intruder invading your home. Treat illness like you would an intruder - command it to go, in the name of Jesus. Speak to migraines and command them to cease. Speak to cancer and command it to flee from you. You have the authority in Jesus to speak to mountains and command them to be cast into the sea. Don't doubt that it's God's will for you to be healed. Trust in His plan. Wait on Him and obtain your victory by faith.

Today's Confession:

Confess His Word: "Father I believe you have a plan to prosper me in my health. I reject the enemy's plan of sickness and disease. I receive your plan of divine health into my heart. I believe I receive healing by the precious blood of your Son Jesus."

Today's Inspirational Quote:

"As I see it, every day you do one of two things: build health or produce disease in yourself." - Adelle Davis

A List of Healing Scriptures for Confession and Meditation

Psalm 118:17

Deuteronomy 28:1-14, 61

Deuteronomy 30:19-20

Psalm 91:16

Psalm 103:3

Isaiah 41:10

Jeremiah 30:17

3 John 2

Matthew 8:2-3

1 Timothy 1:7

Nahum 1:9

Philippians 2:13

I Peter 2:24

Joel 3:10

I John 3:21-22

Romans 4:17-20

Proverbs 4:20-23

Deuteronomy 7:15

Matthew 8:17

I Kings 8:56 2

John 10:10

Hebrews 10:23

Hebrews 10:35

Hebrews 11:11

Revelations 12:1

Hebrews 13:8

Exodus 15:26

Matthew 18:18-19

Exodus 23:25

Isaiah 53:4-5

Ephesians 6:10-17

Your feedback is important. If you enjoyed this book and think the message should be spread, please take a moment to leave a comment at Amazon.

God Bless.

Book 4

Get Off Your Knees And Do Something:

17 Things to do after you pray

Lynn R Davis

Lynnrdavis.com

Copyright © 2012
Lynn R. Davis

All rights reserved. No part of this book may be reproduced or transmitted in any form or by any means without written permission from the author.

Printed in USA by Lynn R. Davis

Dedication

This book is dedicated to God. Lord, you are my source and my strength. You are the one constant source of love and joy in my life. I love you, Lord, with all of my heart. Thank you for placing a dream in my heart and helping me to make it a reality.

Table of Contents

Introduction 4
1-Forgive the unforgivable 5
2-Be thankful when you feel ungrateful 7
3-Sit still and listen 9
4-Get dressed 11
5-Go the other way 14
6-Straighten your face 16
7-Stop making yourself sick.............17
8-Separate yourself 19
9-Lose the so-called friends.............20
10-Speak no evil 22
11-Confessions it 24
12-Listening praise music 27
13-Spend time with Him...................28
14-Rip off the Roof............................31
15-Laugh It Up 33
16-Give yourself away 35
17-Get Started 37

Introduction

It takes more than prayer.

"Just pray and leave it alone", is nonsense. Nothing and I do mean nothing, gets accomplished by *just praying*. You have to get off your knees and do something.

There's more to gaining victory than just praying…so much more. Yes, yes, I know. 1 Thessalonians 5:17 is great. And we should pray without ceasing. I got that part. It's the other part, the "what to do after you pray" part that I somehow missed.

Faith is the key. Prayer is the door. But, once the door opens, you must be courageous enough to walk through it. It takes guts and action to get your prayers answered. Do you have guts? Of course you do.

It won't be easy. You'll want to quit because it looks like nothing is happening. But stay encouraged. Let the joy of the Lord be your strength and He will show up. He has to because He promised and He cannot lie.

1

Forgive the unforgivable

After my divorce, I was angry and bitter. Ii felt like I'd invested years of my life in a toxic relationship only to watch it fall apart. Every night, I cried myself to sleep.

I hated him, I hated them and I hated everyone else involved. I wished something bad would happen to the people who hurt me. I wanted them to be exposed so that I could feel vindicated. I was hurting and I wanted God to do something, but His ways are not our ways.

For months (okay, years) I held this anger and resentment in my heart. I felt that I had a right to hold a grudge—I had been hurt, after all. But, one night in Bible study, God led me to Mark 11:24-25. I knew I had to forgive and let go if I wanted to heal and grow closer to God.

When I prayed, I called out the names of people I hated. Yes, I said hated. I mentioned everyone I could think of. "Lord I forgive _____" and I thank you for forgiving me. And Father I receive healing from anger by faith."

Picture the face of the person who wronged you. Now ask yourself:

* Is _____ worth forfeiting your own forgiveness?
* Is _____ worth my sanity?
* Is _____ worth the time I spend thinking about him/her/it?

As long as you hold that grudge, you're holding that person or thing close to heart. Let it go. Let them go. Let God's love fill that space.

My favorite example of forgiving the unforgivable is Joseph. His own brothers sold him into slavery. But when Joseph finally had chance to pay them back, he didn't. He forgave them.

Stop wasting precious time seeking revenge. Forgive and hand your animosity, grief and anger over to God. So that when you pray, God will forgive you and the flow of blessings will open to you.

Your happiness is the greatest revenge.

2
When you feel ungrateful be thankful

Sometimes when we pray, we are so busy concentrating on ourselves, and the problems we have, that we forget to be thankful.

> *"Do not be anxious about anything, but in everything, by prayer and petition, with thanksgiving, present your requests to God."*
> (Philippians 4:6)

God has stood by you in the past and He continues to do so now. Despite the mess you've gotten yourself into, He has been right there waiting for you to decide change is necessary. Thank Him for that. Whatever you're facing, know that things could have been a whole lot worse. Thank Him for that.

God's mercies are new every morning, you are still here. In spite of your enemies, you are still living and breathing. And as long as you are breathing, you can succeed. With God, you will. Thank Him for that.

> *"Let them give thanks to the LORD for His loving kindness, and for His wonders to the sons of men!"*
> (Psalms 107:8)

Remember: Forgiveness is not for your enemy, it's for you. Holding a grudge blocks God's ability to forgive and bless you. Let it go. Move on and watch God work. Be thankful for what God has already done and what He will do in your future.

3
Sit still and listen

My prayers were microwave conversations with God. I put in my request. Went round and round about how I felt about the issue. And when I was done, I popped up and proceeded to the next task. My prayers were quick, fast and hurried. There was no time allocated to "listening," only time dedicated to asking.

I had a million reasons why I didn't have time to sit still and listen after praying. I was tired, I was sleepy. I had laundry to wash, calls to return and dinner to cook. My son needed help with his homework, or my friend needed advice.

Asking for help with my bills and a new promotion at work was higher on my priority list than listening. I asked. He listened. I pleaded. He listened some more. Then when I was done, prayer time was over. At that point I figured it was up to Him to work it out.

I'd missed it. Prayer is communication. Communication involves dialoguing and listening. You talk, God listens. Then God talks and you listen. I think many people, like me, get so caught up in asking we forget to listen for the answer.

God answers in many ways. He speaks through music, songs, scripture, dreams, ideas, and so on. Sometimes as you sit silently, God may provoke a thought or gently urge you to read a particular scripture. Take time to hear what He has to say. Hear with your heart and Hear with your mind. You'll be glad you did.

4
Get Dressed

Don't forget that you are in battle—a spiritual one. So get dressed for it. Superman had a red and blue suit, Wonder Woman had bracelets that deflected bullets and you have the armor of God.

Alright I'm joking, but consider the concept. They dressed for battle and so should we.

> *"For we wrestle not against flesh and blood, but against principalities, against powers, against the rulers of the darkness of this world, against spiritual wickedness in high places."* (Ephesians 6:12)

The truth of the matter is that Satan is the prince of darkness and he has demons on the earth. Their sole purpose is to torment and defeat Christians. That means that you. Satan heard your prayer, and the last thing he wants is for you to be delivered from your challenge. Misery loves company.

That's why after you pray it seems all hell breaks loose. You pray for stronger church commitment and your car breaks down. Or you pray that your child is delivered from rebellion and, the next thing you know, they get arrested- been there done that. I prayed once that God would bless my finances and I made the commitment to "tithe no matter what."

The hot water heater broke. The heater went out in December. The motor in my refrigerator stopped working. And my car engine started overheating. My cousin hadn't been to church in years. He prayed that he would be more committed to attending church.

The first Sunday he attended, service was wonderful, but on the way home he was in an accident and wrecked his car. He said he wished he'd stayed home.

You can have every intention of succeeding or doing better but things will happen that could hinder you. So after you pray you should intentionally dress for battle, because the enemy will attack. Be ready.

Remember, Jesus came so that you might have "life and have it more abundantly." Regardless of what you are going through, the truth is that you are more than a conqueror; you can do all things through Christ who strengthens you.

Here's what you should know, the armor of God is:

*Vastly superior to anything else you could ever use.

*Stronger than any man's arms or any woman's love.

Your armor protects your heart, mind, body and soul. Your armor will help you stand flat-footed and firm during the battle.

<u>5</u>

Go the other way

You've humbled yourself and you've prayed. You're suited from head to toe. So now what? Well, according to 2 Chronicles 7:14, its time to change direction!

If you allow fear or ungodly advice to guide you, you will end up in the middle of nowhere; alone, out of gas, with no one to call. Sound scary? It is. Look around you—if everything seems foreign, nothing makes sense anymore and you feel desperate or confused, you're going the wrong way.

You're accounts are overdrawn. Bankruptcy is imminent. The kids are out of control. Your relationship is falling apart. It's time to change direction. What's your destination? Whether it's debt freedom, healthy living, prosperity, a restored relationship or something else, God has the directions. But, you have to follow the directions to get where you want to go.

Once you're ready to follow His direction, don't look back. There's nothing to gain from looking back at the destruction in your past. Learn from it and move forward. It doesn't matter how long you've been going in the wrong direction because God's mercies are new every morning. You can start your new journey today. Whatever you were doing that landed you in debt, just change direction.

Leave whomever you need to leave. Stop what you need to stop. Dismiss Repent, change it and move forward. And for peat's sake, don't look back!

6
Straighten Your Face

What does your facial expression like when you're bearing a burden? Have you ever noticed? Do you scowl, frown or pout? When people look at you, do they know right away that something is wrong? Is it written all over your face and you don't have to say a word?

After you pray, stand up straight; change your attitude and fix your face. You have blessed assurance. God has heard you and He will answer your prayer. Your enemy won't understand why you are smiling. And some may even try to remind you how bad your situation is. Ignore them. Don't worry about what "they" think. God is going to answer your prayer, not them.

Smile. You look better when you smile.

7
Stop Making Yourself Sick

I jumped out of bed and walked around the room praying and taking deep breaths. I was having an anxiety attack. It was a scary. The next anxiety attack happened a few weeks later, on the drive home from work.

It felt like I couldn't breathe. I was stressing and I was making myself sick.

I hope you are not in this situation, but if you are, then this chapter is especially for you. You are not imagining things and you are not a hypochondriac. Stress, anger and worry can (and will) make you physically ill. I'm not saying you will never stress. I'm merely encouraging you to find a better way to handle it. Recognize your stress signs.

When I start feeling lightheaded, or I begin to feel neck pain, I immediately know what's happening—those are my stress signs. I catch myself and realize that I'm magnifying my problem over everything else, even my God. I take a deep breath, redirect my thoughts and, if circumstances allow, I may even go for a walk.

Faith Confessions are particularly helpful. I inhale deeply, on the exhale I say something like, "No weapon formed shall prosper" or "God has not given me a spirit of fear." This works for me. Figure out what your stress signs are, find out what works for you and do it.

Cast your cares on the Lord. Stress and worry will make you sick. Find an outlet to reduce stress. Exercising, walking, dancing, meditating—all are just a few ways to reduce stress. Go to the doctor. See a counselor. Do something about it. Just stop making yourself sick.

8
Separate Yourself

God instructed Abraham to leave his homeland, his kinfolk and his immediate family. Can you imagine? You are to leave everyone and everything you know and go to a place that you know nothing about.

God promised Abraham, *"I will make of thee a great nation, and I will bless thee and make thy name great; and thou shalt be a blessing."* God wants to give you greater blessings and success, but perhaps He is asking you to leave the complacency or the distractions of your current life before he can do so.

He won't force you to "come out from among them," but He will bless you if you are obedient. Trust God, He will fulfill His promises. Separate yourself from those people and things that He has asked you to leave and allow Him to lead you into your place of blessings and greatness.

Remember: Wherever God leads you, He will be there too.

9
Lose the so-called friends

"Do not be deceived: 'Evil company corrupts good habits'."
(1 Corinthians 15: 33)

One by one, the fake friendships fall through. When life gets shaky and uncertain, they disappear. Go through a tough time and you'll definitely find out these people are not your friends.

For example, I would NOT consider the following to be true friends.

People who:
- Show up only when you are doing well
- Call only when they need something
- Talk but never listen
- Take but never give

The best thing you can do for people like those described above is cut them loose. Don't make excuses for them. Your energy is better spent investing in and surrounding yourself with real friends. Let the sifting process work. Embrace its benefits- separating toxic relationships from healthy ones. Then focus on the positive ones that support your goals.

I read some place that people who come into our lives are there for a season; a reason; or a lifetime. Those who come for a reason are there to help us during a particular situation or struggle.

People who we know for a season are a temporary part of our lives, as we pass through a certain phase. Others (who I consider real friends) are in our lives for a lifetime. They are blessings from above and they are with you no matter what, through thick and thin.

Recognize who the people are in your life and understand that not all of them will be, or should be, lifetime friends.

10
Speak no evil

Speaking positively, when things are not going well, initiates the process of positive change. The biblical principle behind this is: "calling those things that be not, as though they were."

As believers we should be very careful how we respond to even the simplest challenges in our lives by guarding what we say and being aware of what others are saying about us.

The Bible tells us in Job that Satan roams the earth in search of people to destroy. Satan listens for words of despair and unbelief, and when he hears them he swiftly goes to work making those words a reality. Romans 10:17 tells us that faith comes by hearing, and hearing by the word of God.

The words that you hear continually will penetrate your mind and you will begin to meditate on them. This is why God tells us to meditate on His word day and night. You meditate on His word so that you know the truth. And once that truth is in your heart it will manifest in your speech.

Speak the word over your situation. Speak victory, peace, and love, regardless of what you see. Confess scriptures not morbid statistics and advice from unsaved critics. At first you will have to work at it. But as you practice speaking faith filled words on purpose, you'll begin to do it automatically.

11
Confess It

I'm happy to share these with you. I sincerely hope that they are a blessing to you. Use them as examples to create your own confessions for your own unique situations. Remember, speak them, believe them and you will see results.

Healing Confession

Father, I thank you for your healing power. I declare that I am healed by the stripes of Jesus and made whole. Your word says, if I diligently seek You, You will hear the commandments and none of these diseases shall be on me. No sickness or disease shall lord over my body. My body is a temple of Christ. It belongs to You and I commit my health and healing over to You. I receive my health in Jesus' name. (Acts 14:9 * Isaiah 53:5 * Luke 4:8 * James 5:16 *
1 Peter 2:24)

Confession for Favor

I thank You Lord, for Your mercy and grace toward me. I declare that daily I am growing in stature and in favor with God and man. I am a good person and therefore I obtain favor from the Lord. Thank You, Father, that I love instruction and knowledge. I know that promotion comes from You and that all grace abounds toward me, and no good thing is withheld from me, because I walk uprightly. (Proverbs 12:2 * Jeremiah 26:19 * Luke 2:52)

Confession for Courage
Lord, Your word says that you have not given me a spirit of fear, but of love, power and a sound mind. I thank You Lord, that I am strong and of good courage. I do not fear and I am not afraid. I am not afraid of their faces, for I know that You are with me and will never leave me. You will protect me and You will put your foot on the necks of my enemy. In Jesus' name, Amen. (Deuteronomy 31:6 * 2 Timothy 1:7 * Hebrews 13:5 * Joshua 10:25)

Confession for Child
Father, I thank You that my child is a righteous man/woman of God, whose steps are ordered by the Lord. My child makes wise decisions and will not follow the voice of strangers; instead, he will flee from the stranger. My child has the favor of God and man, and all that my child sets his/her hand to do shall prosper. In Jesus' name, Amen. (Psalms 37:23 * John 10:5 * Luke 2:52)

Confession for Peace

Lord, Your word says that I shall both lie down in peace and sleep, for You alone, O Lord, make me dwell in safety. Your word also says that in You I will have peace, and peace of God, which surpasses all understanding, will guard my heart and mind through Christ Jesus. Lord, I thank You for peaceful rest and sleep. In Jesus' name, Amen. (Psalms 4:8 * John 16:33 * Ephesians 2:4 * Romans 5:1)

There are so many more confessions that I could add, but I hope that these few will give you an idea of how to create your own by using the words of scripture.

Remember: Be encouraged and know that the word of God will not return void, but it will accomplish what it says. Confess it boldly. Confess it often.

12

Listen to Praise Music

Music has been found to have an effect on the thinking process and it can affect the listener's mood. Research shows listening to positive music makes it easier for people to perform difficult tasks.

If you find yourself in an odd place and don't have access to music, sing a song instead. Paul and Silas sang songs and praised God while they were locked in prison! The foundations started shaking and the shackles fell off.

Whatever the prison you are bound in, if you just sing praises unto the Lord, I promise you that God will move and release you from your bondage. No jail cell or shackle can hold you. God has the master key. So don't sit there and mope and sulk like I used to do. Get up turn on some praise music and dance like David did!

13
Spend time with Him

Instead of spending your time reading fiction novels, chatting online or obsessing over social networking posts, spend some time with God. Get to know Him. Read His word and seek His wisdom.

Some people get up early in the morning to pray. Others pray three times a day. There is no single "correct" method or process to get to know your God.

I find that getting up a little earlier in the morning to pray really does get my day started on the right foot. But, I admit, because I'm not a morning person, my study time is usually during lunch or in the evenings. Start where you are. Don't feel like you have to get up at 6:00 a.m. every morning or read the entire Bible in 90 days. Start by reading a memory verse each morning and reflect on it.

Think about what the verse is saying and how it applies to your life. Ask God for revelation and understanding. The more you do this, the more you will understand who God is and what His plan is for you. This is your journey. Set your own pace. Read the word. Meditate on it. Ask God for understanding and wisdom. You don't have to do what everyone else is doing. Do what works for you. But whatever you do, get started.

Here are three things to do when preparing to spend time with God:

- Turn off the telephone or ringer. Trust me; the minute you get started praising, worshiping, reading your Bible or meditating, the phone will ring. Turn it off.
- Lock the door to your room if you are able. This prevents someone unexpectedly walking in to ask you about their lost car keys or to complain that their favorite toy is missing.
- Make it known. Let people in your house know that you are designating time to spend with God and that you should not be interrupted.
- Have everything you need handy. Be sure your pen, favorite Bible, worship CD, journal or anything else you think you will need during this time is near at hand. You don't want to have to go the car to get your Bible in the middle of your meditation.

Spending time with God strengthens your relationship with Him. Any relationship suffers when the parties involved don't devote quality time to sustain the bond between them.

14
Rip Off the Roof If You Have To

Giving up is not an option. Because you have already completed Language Therapy 101, you know that phrases like *"I give up"* are not acceptable. While you are waiting for your breakthrough, you may endure some challenges. And there will be times that you will need the help of others. As such the people around you should be people you can rely on in tough times.

There's a story about a paralyzed man in Mark 2. The man and his friends heard that Jesus was at a particular meeting place. When they arrived, the building was packed and there seemed to be no way for them to get close to Jesus. But, they were persistent. They sincerely wanted to help their friend receive his healing. The situation appeared impossible, they didn't give up.

The four friends climbed on top of the building and tore a hole in the roof so that they could lower their friend down to Jesus. Because of their faith and perseverance, their friend received his healing. The paralytic's situation seemed hopeless. The crowd was huge. Jesus was far away. There was no obvious solution to the problem. But, he didn't give up.

You cannot give up just because the answer does not seem obvious or because the task appears impossible. You have to be willing to remove whatever is standing between you and your breakthrough. You have to be willing to rip off the roof.

God began a good work in you and He is faithful to complete it. Every step you make in the direction of your dreams and goals brings you closer to realizing them. At your appointed time, you will receive your harvest. When your friends, family and enemies see that God has delivered you, they will be amazed. That amazement will increase their desire to know your God. Your harvest will be a blessing to your entire family.

Bottom line: don't let anything stand in the way of your breakthrough. Keep working toward your goal no matter whom or what tries to stop you.

15
Laugh It Up!

My son was staying at his dads for the weekend, so I decided to rent a bunch of movies, put on my favorite PJs and curl up. No tear-jerkers that required a box of Kleenex. Scary movies—no thank you! I don't do those and my boss's attitude was horror for one week.

I needed to laugh and laugh hard. I went to the video store and picked up a hand full of my favorite comedies. They didn't disappoint me one bit. I laughed till my belly ached. There's something about laughter that instantly creates a burst of life and positive energy. That's why I love laughing and I love making people laugh. I truly believe "laughter is the best medicine" in the majority of cases. No matter how bad things are, you can always find solace in laughter.

In 1996, our mom passed away suddenly. She was home that morning and by late evening she was gone. A blood clot traveled to her lung and she stopped breathing on the way to the emergency room.

That was a very difficult and painful time for both my father and us kids. I was an adult, but my youngest sisters were only 7 and 10. Before and after the funeral, I remember sitting around talking about some of the quirky things my mother did when she was alive. Someone would recall something funny and we'd all burst into laughter.

Even though we were in pain, we still laughed. The laughter had a kind of calming effect, almost like a like a warm bath. It seemed to soothe away the stress. No matter how bad things look for you, laugh and laugh often.

16
Give Yourself Away

After you pray, make a commitment to sow. I don't just mean giving money—for some, giving money is simple. Writing a check is the easy way out. You write, sign and drop it in a bucket, then move on. You expend no real effort or suffer any inconvenience.

Granted, giving monetary gifts is admirable and I can think of dozens of organizations that would love to receive them, but let's think outside the money box. Instead of taking the easy way out, consider giving outside of your check-writing comfort zone. Think of ways to help others that require you to give of yourself, not just your money. Commit to sow your time and talent as opposed to your dollars and cents.

I know it can seem like a burden, especially when you have so much on your plate already. If you don't understand sowing, you will mistakenly assume that the person on the receiving end is getting the better deal. You have to change the way you think about giving (sowing). As the giver, you are blessed far greater than the person you're giving to.

When you sow seeds, whether they are seeds of money, finances or time, you begin a powerful principle of seed time harvest time. You plant seeds that will produce a harvest. The exciting part is you never know how great of a harvest you will receive—only God knows.

Use your God given talents and resources to help others achieve their goals. Volunteer in your church, give to charity and pray for the sick. Bless the homeless and be a companion for the lonely. Maybe the person who has been assigned to help you is tied to your ministry assignment. Perhaps your gift is the key that will unlock your breakthrough. Unless you sow, you will never know. Find a way to be a blessing. You will be blessed in return.

17
Get Started

"Where should I start?" That depends. Which one of the principles do you feel most concerned about? If you are constantly battling negative thoughts and language, that's where you should start.

Whatever principle you choose start with will be a blessing to you. Just get started. In the words of Calvin Coolidge, "We cannot start everything at once, but we can start one thing at once." Starting is truly half the battle. You can do it. Keep the faith and trust God that He will always be there for you during your journey.

If you enjoyed this collection and think it's a message that could bless others, please take a moment to leave a comment on Amazon. Your comment may be what encourages another believer to read.

Visit **http://lynnrdavis.com** read my latest blog posts and leave your feedback, ask questions, or make comments.

Made in the USA
San Bernardino, CA
14 November 2017